For Sue,

With gratitude for the
glorify God in song.

Grace & peace,

Emily

GLORIFY

Reclaiming the Heart of Progressive Christianity

EMILY C. HEATH

Emily C. Heath

Cleveland
The Pilgrim Press

D0291615

To Heidi | *who every day teaches me just a little more about glorifying God.*

The Pilgrim Press, 700 Prospect Avenue, Cleveland, Ohio 44115
thepilgrimpress.com
© 2016 by Emily C. Heath

Scripture quotations, unless otherwise noted, are from the New Revised Standard Version of the Bible, © 1989 by the Division of Christian Education of the National Council of Churches of Christ in the United States of America, and are used by permission. Changes have been made for inclusivity.

Printed in the United States of America on acid-free paper

19   18   17   16   15   5   4   3   2   1

ISBN: 978-0-8298-2029-4

CONTENTS

Acknowledgments

I am profoundly grateful to so many for their encouragement, support, and affirmation through the years, and especially during the time I was writing this book. There are a few in particular to whom I would like to say "thank you":

To the professors, pastors, chaplains, and others who taught me about faith, both inside and outside of classrooms and pulpits, particularly at Emory University and Columbia Theological Seminary.

To the many other clergy members, particularly my colleagues in the United Church of Christ and Presbyterian Church (USA), with whom I have been honored to serve.

To Tina Villa of Pilgrim Press, who encouraged me to turn a blog post into a book, and who guided me through the process of writing my first book.

To the fabulous people of the Congregational Church in Exeter, who give me the privilege of serving as their senior pastor. I am grateful in particular for the ways they support and encourage my writing.

ACKNOWLEDGMENTS

To the Rev. Dr. Carol Pitts, mentor extraordinaire, who is never short on good and faithful advice.

To my family, both my loving family of origin and my superb chosen family of friends, who are constant sources of joy, strength, and support.

To my brilliant and beautiful wife, who, by the time this book is released, will be the Rev. Heidi Carrington Heath. It was always you.

But most of all, I offer this work with profound gratitude to God, whose grace has been given to me beyond measure. I pray that my words here may only bring glory to God.

Feast of Christ the King, 2015
Exeter, New Hampshire

PART ONE

FINDING OUR PURPOSE

I

The Next Big Thing

THROWING THE BABY JESUS OUT WITH THE BATHWATER

"So, now that we have LGBTQ equality in the mainline church, what are we going to do? What's the next big thing?"

I get asked that question from time to time. The tide seems to have turned in many ways when it comes to the inclusion of people of all genders and sexualities in both our churches and our country. Doors to ordination are opening, marriages are being blessed, and the church is growing more comfortable with talking openly about sexuality and gender.

And so the question is already being asked by some: What shall we work on next? What big issue does the church need to face?

I have a few thoughts. First, I don't think the church is anywhere near the end of discussions about full inclusion for LGBTQ people. Yes, we are far better off than we were ten years ago, and even further from where we were before that, but we aren't close to being completely inclusive yet. (By the way, we're not quite done with debates over the role of women or confronting our complicity in racism, either.)

But, for purposes of discussion, let's just say it is time for the mainline church to start looking for the "next big thing" that will unite us in purpose and divide us in debate. What will it be?

As I said, I have some ideas. Caring for the environment is on the top of the list. Responding to growing numbers of refugees and to other humanitarian crises is too. So is interfaith understanding. And I don't think it will be too long until the church seriously begins to discuss economic inequalities. There are a lot of possibilities.

I was thinking about that recently. I was sitting with other clergy from my denomination, talking about my views on why it's important for progressive ministers to be able to talk about our faith, and about what Christ means to us. I was talking about discipleship, and why it matters for our progressive church, and about how we've lost so much of our theological heritage, and our language of faith. That's when the question came, part curious, part suspect:

"But what about social justice? Doesn't that matter to you?"

The person who asked that question didn't know me. They didn't know that for more than twenty now years I have been openly gay. They didn't know about the times when anonymous, antigay hate letters showed up in my church's mailbox during my last call, or about how I'd grown up in a place where being gay could literally get you blown up, or about how my wife, Heidi, and I had needed to file separate federal tax returns even after we were married.

They also didn't know about the times my faith had compelled me to take action. I could have told them about how a group of us had stood in the New York State Capitol building for the better part of a week as right-wing Christians rallying against equal marriage had yelled at us that we were going to hell. I've gone a few rounds in the social justice arena.

But the person who questioned me? They aren't alone. So many times when I talk about why the church needs to reclaim discipleship, starting with asking ourselves, "Who do I believe that Jesus is to me?" even my progressive

Christian friends look at me sideways. Those of us who ask these questions in progressive faith settings often find ourselves being told that we are too dogmatic, too conservative, or too focused on what doesn't matter.

The problem is, I think it does matter. I think it matters more than we know.

I often worry that the progressive side of the mainline church has begun to define ourselves not by our affirmations, but by our repudiations. When compared with our more conservative siblings in the faith we are so quick to say, "We aren't like that." We proclaim "not all Christians" with ease. But when it comes to talking about what we *do* believe, we often find we lack the words.

I sometimes worry that we progressive Christians put the cart before the horse when it comes to social justice. It's not that I believe we are advocating for the wrong things; it's that I believe we sometimes advocate for the wrong reasons, acting first and then wedging theological meaning in later as an afterthought.

I am glad, for instance, that churches stand up against antigay measures. I wish more would. But I want us to talk about why our Christian convictions are compelling us to do so.

I give thanks for every church member who stands and protests against the death penalty, but I want us to be able to talk about what the crucified Christ taught us about the value of human life.

I respect every Christian who holds a placard in front of the White House and speaks about climate change, but I wish I heard more about how God created the world and called it good, and why that's why we can't be silent.

Even when I walk into a voting booth, I take my faith with me. When I cast my votes, I do so in accordance with what the gospel has taught me. I cannot separate the two. And I give thanks for that.

But before I got to this place, I first had to become a disciple. I had to read the gospel for myself and want to follow the Christ I read about there. Only then could I go about the work of living my faith in the public arena, both in the larger church and in the world.

And so when people ask me what the "next big thing" in the church will be, I tell them this: discipleship.

There are a lot of reasons why the church doesn't wield the influence we once had in the public sphere, but I think the main one is this: we have forgotten our foundation. We have forgotten what it means to be disciples. And people can see through us.

Few people are interested in joining just another public advocacy group, and those who are can find far more effective ones. The progressive church is not the "Democratic Party at Prayer," to borrow a phrase, and if we continue to lose our theological literacy and our ability to talk about our faith, that's all we will end up being. Without a bedrock of belief, the whole enterprise of church-based social justice will crumble.

Add to that my biggest fear, which is that the "next big thing" for the progressive church is attempting to "save" ourselves. For some reason the majority of our denominational conversations these days seem to be about how to preserve our institutions and legacies, even if we try to disguise that fact by claiming we are trying something radical and new. The fact of the matter is, until we somehow refocus on the heart of our faith, we are doing the ecclesiastical equivalent of simply rearranging deck chairs on the Titanic.

But that doesn't have to happen anymore.

It's time for progressive Christians to claim discipleship. It's time to get radical, not about our politics or our policies, but about our faith. It's time to stop throwing the baby Jesus out with the bathwater, and start putting the horse before the cart. It's time to remember what, and whom, we worship, and to develop the language of faith.

And it's time to see our social justice work as a natural product of our discipleship, not something that competes with it for the church's time.

Only then, when we have gone back to the source and found what ultimately binds us together with God and with one another, can we go out and find the next, next big thing. Whenever that happens, we will be better for it. In fact, we just may find that when it comes to changing the world for the better, the Gospel of Why We Are Different from Other Christians can't hold a candle to the Gospel of Jesus Christ.

CHOOSING LIFE OR DEATH

When I wrote the words you just read, they were meant to serve only as a blog post. They resonated with many, and then ended up being reprinted in an issue of the United Church of Christ's *Still Speaking* magazine. I was then asked to expand on them in workshops and sermons.

Before long it became clear that there was a deep hunger in my own denomination, as well as in many of the other denominations that make up what we once called the "mainline church." In the latter half of the twentieth century many of those mainline churches, like the UCC, Presbyterian Church (USA), Evangelical Lutheran Church in America, Episcopal Church, Disciples, American Baptists, many United Methodists, and others became the base of the progressive Christian movement.

That is something of which we are, rightfully, very proud of in our denominations. We've helped to lend powerful voices of faith to a variety of movements: civil rights, peace, women's rights, LGBTQ rights, anti-death penalty work, poverty alleviation, and more. We have faithfully done our best to mediate between gospel and culture.

And yet, as denominations we are dying. I say that without panic because I believe the church is far greater than the sum of our denominations. The reality is, if the church is truly the body of Christ, then it cannot die.

But the fact remains that the former mainline church is at a crisis point. If we continue our current rate of decline, our denominations will be extinct within many of our lifetimes. In fact, the Pew Research Center found in 2014 that only 14.7 percent of American adults are a part of a mainline Protestant denomination, down 3.4 percent in only seven years.[1]

The numbers get worse when you look generationally. Only 11 percent of millennial young adults identify as mainline Protestants, compared to 26 percent of their grandparents' generation. My own denomination, the United Church of Christ, has gone from more than two million members in 1957 (the year two denominations merged to form the current one) to less than one million today. And each of the other mainline denominations can tell a similar story.

At the same time, more conservative traditions are seeing growth, or at least declining at a much slower rate. Evangelical Christians saw only a 0.9 percent decline in the same seven-year period mentioned above. For Orthodox Christians and Mormons that rate was only 0.1 percent.

But what is most interesting is what traditions (and nontraditions) are growing. Islam, Judaism, and Buddhism all saw modest gains in the United States. And atheists and agnostics grew at a rate of 1.5 percent and 1.6 percent, respectively. But the greatest movement? That came from a group that we are just now starting to hear more about: the "nones," who are those with no particular faith or religious tradition. They grew 3.7 percent, or more than we lost.

Mainline Christians have a hand in that. We have the worst "retention rate" when it comes to our young people; 45 percent, less than half, of our youth continue to claim our tradition into young adulthood. That number dips to 37 percent, or just over a third, when you look at millennials. More and more of our youth are graduating from high school, stepping out into the world, and becoming "nones."

At the same time, more young people as a whole are being raised outside of organized religion completely. Parents who have been disillusioned by the church are seeing less value in raising their children in the faith. Others, driven by an increasingly difficult balance between work and family life, take Sunday as their one "day off" when they are able to stay home or spend the day with their kids.

Add to that the scheduling issues. Fifty years ago there were no Little League games on Sunday mornings, and the stores stayed closed. But while we like to complain about Sunday soccer practice, the reality is that those practices would have never been moved to Sunday mornings had the church not already lost so many of its faithful. Sunday soccer did not kill church attendance. Sunday soccer sprang up when people stopped finding something more worthwhile in our houses of faith, and instead looked to something new.

Like I said, I share this news without panic. I deeply love my denomination, as well as the other denominations that make up the mainline traditions. I sit on the board of directors of the UCC, and I would not be who I am without my education at a United Methodist college and a Presbyterian seminary. I would be sad to see any of these denominations cease to exist.

But I would not necessarily lose any hope because of it.

As I said, denominations are not synonymous with the church. They help us to make meaning of our traditions, and to tie us together in fellowship and ministry in more formal ways, but in the end they are replaceable. By the time I retire, somewhere in late 2040s, God willing, I suspect that the denominational landscape in the United States will look radically different than it does today.

Again, this is not bad news. Compulsory Christianity is done. No longer will your neighbors come to church on Sunday morning simply because it is expected of them. Our congregations will not be filled by those whose internalized religious guilt or sense of familial obligation drives them into the pews (except maybe on Christmas Eve or Easter Sunday).

This means that the people who come through your doors and stay are there not because they have to be, but because they want to be. And that is very good news. I would rather have a congregation of one hundred people committed to walking on a journey of faith together than a packed sanctuary of five hundred people who won't think about God again until next Sunday morning. The church of the willing will always be able to go deeper than the church of obligatory attendees.

But when the willing come to our doors (or, if they are already there, decide to stay) we have to do some deep reflection on ourselves, on who we are, and on who we will be in the world. Our timing is good. The late Phyllis Tickle argued that every five hundred years the church goes through some sort of large-scale reformation. As we approach the five-hundredth anniversary of Martin Luther's 95 theses, we are due for the next.

ARE WE READY FOR RESURRECTION?

For the mainline tradition that has become the progressive Christian movement we have a choice: we can be left behind as a footnote while other traditions and nontraditions grow. Or we can choose resurrection.

The body of Christ knows all about resurrection. It was the Resurrection of Christ that gave birth to this whole movement. And so resurrection should be our natural inclination. But I truly believe it is a choice that progressive Christians are going to have to actively choose. It is one that will require adaptation, redefinition, and more than a little "letting go." And it is one that, above all, will require us to remember who we are, and to whom we belong.

There is a story in the book of Deuteronomy about Moses calling the people to him. They had fled oppression, walked through the Red Sea, wandered for forty years in the wilderness, and worshiped a golden idol they had built for themselves. And yet they were still alive, and they stood ready to enter the promised land.

Before they did, though, Moses asked them to enter into a covenant with God. Moses tells the crowd, "If you obey the commandments of the Lord your God, . . . by walking in God's ways, and observing God's commandments, decrees, and ordinances, then you shall live and become numerous, and the Lord your God will bless you in the land that you are entering to possess. But if your heart turns away and you do not hear, but are led astray to bow down to other gods and serve them, I declare to you today that you shall perish" (Deut. 30:16–17).

He tells them, "Choose life so that you and your descendants may live" (Deut. 30:19).

And so, no matter what the resurrection will look like for progressive Christians, it starts with this: the renewal of our covenant with God, and the turning first to God in all things. Life and death are set before us. For our descendants, for ourselves, and for all of those on whose shoulders we rest, may we choose well.

2

<h1 style="text-align:center">HIDDEN UNDER A BUSHEL</h1>

OUR PUBLIC RELATIONS PROBLEM

I was recently walking back to the office after lunch when I saw a car parked on the street in front of the church. On the back was a bumper sticker: "Too stupid for science? Try religion."

I laughed. But then I found myself grimacing. I know that the suspicion of science is not based in actual Christian belief. My congregation full of educators and scientists disproves that. But the bumper sticker is an accurate summary of what too many people think Christians actually believe.

It gets worse. During the months I wrote this book Kim Davis, the Kentucky county clerk who refused to issue same-sex marriage licenses, sat in jail for contempt of court. On social media, television, and in the newspaper, outraged Christian leaders proclaimed that she was a victim of religious persecution and that Christians in this country are under attack. At the same time conservative Christians ranted that Starbucks had declared a war on Christmas by not writing "Merry Christmas" on their plain red coffee cups. And all the while, Christian governors across the country attempted to close their states' borders to Syrian refugees.

I don't think this is what Christianity is supposed to be about, and if you are reading this book chances are good that you agree. Like me, you might be outraged that your faith has been publicly co-opted by extremist voices. You are perhaps bemoaning the lack of nuance in the public understanding of what it means to be a Christian.

If you are like me, you might be baffled by the fact that a government employee being jailed because she disobeyed a court order to do her job is now somehow seen as a form of religious martyrdom. You might see the irony of turning away refugees in a season when we remember there once was "no room at the inn" for Jesus' family. Or, at the very least, you might want to just get a cup of coffee without having to worry what the cup says.

And, like me, you might think that Christians have a bit of a public relations problem.

I know what it's like to be on the other side of that. I grew up in what Flannery O'Connor called the "Christ-haunted South." Conservative Baptist denominations were all around us. Evangelical and fundamentalist megachurches built towering sanctuaries. The largest national ex-gay ministry at the time was based in my hometown. And nearly everyone I knew went to church.

Except for me.

I was an early "none," especially given my geographic context. Born at the tail end of generation X, to a family with both mainline Protestant and Roman Catholic roots, religion was left up to each of my parents' kids to decide.

What I knew about Christians was mostly what I heard from my conservative evangelical classmates. They despised abortion, "loved the sinner but hated the sin" when it came to LGBTQ folks, taught that women should "graciously submit" to men, and believed that all those who had not been "saved" were going straight to hell.

They also sometimes turned off all their lights and put signs about damnation on their doors at Halloween, rather than give out the devil's candy. So, you know, not exactly a group I was in a hurry to join.

But I always knew there was something deeper out there. I had some sense of the divine even at an early age. I prayed, though I always felt I wasn't doing it "right." And more than anything I wondered if my class-mates were right, and if I really was going to hell.

My senior year of high school a history teacher was trying to illus-trate the ways religious diversity was present in the United States. He wrote a list of Christian denominations on the board, and added a line for the few Jewish students. He then went from student to student asking for us to tell him our family's religion.

Lots of Baptists, Presbyterians, Methodists, and Assembly of God members later, he came to me. And I didn't know how to answer.

"Well, some Presbyterians. Some Congregationalists. Some Catholics."

"I'm going to need one answer."

I hesitated before admitting I didn't have one. I was the only one in my class.

That afternoon I drove my car to the church that seemed the furthest away from the megachurch on the outskirts of town. I made an appoint-ment to talk to an Episcopal priest about being baptized. And in my last semester of high school, without telling many of my friends, I received both baptism and confirmation.

In college I found myself drawn to the progressive Christian campus ministry, and to the liberal Presbyterian church right off campus. This led to three years of seminary and ordination as a Presbyterian minister. After eight years of ministry in the Presbyterian denomination, as the full inclusion of LGBTQ people was still being debated, I transferred my or-dination to the United Church of Christ.

I tell you this because I have always found my background as a former "none" useful to understanding church growth, and the lack thereof. Now that "nones" are the fastest growing religious demographic in our country, I find myself drawing more and more on my experience when I think about how to best welcome people to church, and how to embrace them as fellow travelers on the journey of faith.

For me, walking into the doors of the church was like walking into the clubhouse of a group that I had mostly known to be hostile to people like me. I stepped into the pew unsure of whether or not I would be welcome. And I felt ashamed and hid in a back row when I didn't know things as simple as the Lord's Prayer.

But I was also lucky. When I came out at the age of eighteen, one of the first people I told was my college chaplain, a wonderfully progressive United Methodist minister who offered me nothing but acceptance and affirmation. During college I lived in a southern city with a host of open and affirming churches, and I found steadfast Christian mentors. Later, in seminary, I learned what it was to embrace a nuanced and progressive Christian faith.

This happened because I somehow turned away from the loud messages of the more conservative churches that surrounded me, and instead was drawn by the quiet, insistent voice of the progressive mainline church.

But many of my friends were not so lucky. In college I watched friends of mine come out to evangelical Christian families and then be disowned. Others found churches that spoke to them musically, or through the sermons, but also ridiculed their belief in evolution. Others found judgment for everything from living together with a fiancée to using birth control.

It's no wonder that many people think Christians are judgmental, antigay, antiwomen, antichoice, antiscience extremists. So much of what they have experienced in church has been just that.

Even if people have not experienced it themselves, they have heard about it on the news. When talk shows want someone to offer the "Christian perspective" they far too often call up someone with extremist views who will make for good television. The "religious liberty" and "religious persecution" red herrings of the past decade have further hurt the perception of Christianity in the public mind by cementing the idea that all Christians oppose what the majority of Americans now accept.

It is a rare "none" who dares to venture into the doors of a church given the portrayal of religious belief in our country. Add to that the fact that today's mainline tradition is smaller than it was even when I was in high school, and the chance that a seeker will stumble into a progressive congregation is tinier than ever.

But say someone does come through our doors? What happens then?

Unlike evangelical churches that place an emphasis on "making" and "equipping" disciples, and that see every day as a day in the "mission field," progressive churches are notoriously bad at talking about what it means to be a Christian. The statistic from the last chapter, which shows that only just more than a third of our youth claim our tradition as young adults, bears this out. If we can't even engage and excite the faith of the young people we have from birth, how can we hope to attract newcomers later in life?

HIDDEN UNDER A BUSHEL

The future is not hopeless, but it does demand a change in the way we operate. And the best illustration I know for what we are going to have to do comes from a hymn many of us just think of as a children's song.

"This Little Light of Mine" is one of the most deceptively simple songs around. The words are repetitive and easy. And yet, the message resonates at any age. We each have light to shine, and the song encourages us to defiantly let it do just that.

The verse that speaks most to the formerly mainline church is this one: "Hide it under a bushel? No! I'm gonna let it shine."

The words reflect a story told in several places in the Gospels. Jesus tells his disciples, "No one after lighting a lamp puts it under the bushel basket, but on the lamp stand, and it gives light to all in the house. In the same way, let your light shine before others, so that they may see your good works and give glory to God in heaven" (Matt. 5:15–16).

In other words, if you have something capable of lighting up your whole house, why would you ever want to hide that light? The only logical thing to do is to place it in the center of your home, so that everything will be transformed by its light. At its brightest, that light will fill not just our homes, but the world as well.

We don't do this well in the progressive church. Too often we leave our light under the bushel, and I truly believe the reason why is that we are afraid.

First, we are afraid of being seen as anything like other Christians. For all the reasons listed above, those of us who have more progressive outlooks on the world are often in the position of having to defend our involvement in an organization that has been deeply hurtful to many. Often that includes people who are our closest friends.

We may also be asked to explain our beliefs to incredulous others, and sometimes we find the questioner already believes they know what we will say. Explaining the nuances of faith to a critical acquaintance at a dinner party can be a losing proposition from the start. Sometimes it feels much easier to keep quiet, and ask someone to pass the potatoes.

More often than not, though, our fear comes not from external voices but internal ones. As much as we are afraid of sharing our light with others, we are more afraid of what the light will show us. And above all, we are afraid of how we will then have to change.

Our public relations problem stems only in small part from the co-opting of the name "Christian" by intolerant and fundamentalist voices. The hard truth is that our public relations problem stems from a faith problem. Our faith problem. We have to admit that.

The time has never been more perfect for progressive Christianity. An entire generation of unchurched and marginally churched young people is rising to adulthood. And though the phrase "spiritual but not religious" continues to have its day, there is a sense that more and more people are finding that it is, in the words of Lillian Daniel, "not enough."

As curious seekers look for the community, ritual, and, yes, structure, they are not just looking in the church. A yoga studio may provide all of those things, for example. But chances are good that seekers might just remember where their grandparents went every Sunday, and decide to check it out. Or they'll get brave enough to enter the doors of that big building on Main Street for the first time and take a look around.

When they do, what will they find? That the light has been hidden under a bushel? Or that someone has left a light on for them?

THE E-WORD

Evangelism.

What are you picturing right now? Missionaries in matching outfits knocking at your front door? A guy thumping a Bible on a street corner? The classmate who cornered you and talked to you about "accepting Jesus Christ as your personal Lord and savior"?

Now how are you feeling?

Uncomfortable? Frustrated? Maybe even a little angry?

You're not alone. Aggressive proselytizing and emotional manipulation are troubling to say the least, but they are not the same as evangelism. They are caricatures of it at best, and active detriments to it at worst. Because of these methods, the word "evangelism" gets a bad name, especially in the progressive church.

And yet, I am going to ask you to become evangelists.

If you are still reading and haven't closed this book for good yet, bear with me. Because as much as the "e-word" and its close relative "evangelical" pushes many of our buttons, I want to make a case for not conceding these important words to the Christian Right.

The word "evangelical" comes from the Greek word transliterated as *euangelion*, which means "good news." For centuries "evangelical" meant not a certain set of political beliefs, but rather the deep faith conviction that God loves us beyond measure and with certain grace.

It's the reason why the relatively progressive Evangelical Lutheran Church in America claims the word in its name. It's why one of the predecessor denominations of the very progressive United Church of Christ was called the Evangelical and Reformed Church. It's the history that has allowed many of our traditions' theologians to claim the word "evangelical" in their work as a message of hope and transcendence.

Historically, the term has nothing to do with hitting people over the head with a Bible, loud tent revival preachers, or going door to door looking for converts. It does not dictate a specific worship style with rock bands and big screens. It has nothing to do with denouncing gay rights, subjugating women, or denying that evolution ever happened.

It just has to do with this: God's love for us, especially as found in the example of Jesus Christ, and our commitment to not keep the good news of God's love to ourselves. Nothing more.

I sometimes describe myself as a liberal evangelical. I'm sad that the public understanding of that word "evangelical" forces me to use a qualifier, but so be it. I believe in spreading the good news of God's love to all. But how I hope to do that looks very different from what most (at least in our North American context) might expect from an evangelical.

To me, evangelism looks like this: marching in the local gay pride parade, growing vegetables to donate to the local food pantry, advocating for fair labor practices, working for peace, protesting racial injustice, providing good quality health care to those who don't have it, and so much more.

All of those things help to spread the good news of God's love. All of those things are evangelism. We do them not just because we want to be good people, but more importantly because we are God's people.

Every Christian should be doing the work of evangelism. No Christian should be allowing the work of evangelism to be co-opted by a more vocal and less inclusive branch of our larger faith. The love of God is our light too, and it's okay to take it out from underneath the bushel and to let our light shine.

ATTRACTION, NOT PROMOTION

With all of this in mind, when we are talking about evangelism it's important to make sure we clear up one popular misconception: evangelism is not about church growth.

We do not do the work of evangelism in order to recruit new members for the team. This is not about adding to our membership rolls. And if the only time your church talks about evangelism is as a way to get more money in the offering plates and "save the church," trust me when I say it just won't happen. People will walk into the doors of your church and see the ulterior motivations from a mile away.

The point of sharing the good news is just this: to share the good news.

We don't do it to get something out of it for ourselves. We don't do it so that we will have more members than the megachurch down the block. And we for sure don't do it to save our buildings, or keep things the way they used to be.

But, if we are consistent in our sharing of God's love for all, and if we are doing it for the right reasons, something surprising will happen to our churches: they will grow.

I mean that both in terms of numbers of engaged people, but also in terms of the spiritual lives of those people. Growth is the natural reaction that happens when a living thing is planted in good soil. It is the organic byproduct of rooting ourselves in what Paul Tillich called the "ground of our being," or God and God's love.

Most people have heard of the Twelve Steps of Alcoholics Anonymous, and other recovery programs. But fewer have heard of their cousin, the Twelve Traditions. These are the principles that people in recovery try to implement in their life together. And one of them in particular is relevant to any discussion of church growth.

Tradition Eleven states that "our public relations policy is based on attraction rather than promotion." That concept of "attraction, not promotion" is a powerful one. Think about AA. There are no AA commercials, newspaper ads, or web banners for the organization itself. The very principles of AA forbid advertising. And yet, almost everyone knows of AA.

Why? Part of the reason has to do with AA's presence in the popular culture, in books, TV, and films. But mostly it has to do with the fact that, one person at a time, lives have been changed by the program. After starting with just two people only eighty years ago, AA is now estimated to have 1.2 million members in the United States alone. (To put that in perspective, that's more than some mainline denominations.)

AA has grown not because of aggressive ad campaigns and corporate rebranding, but because members who have achieved sustained sobriety attract those who are looking for the same. AA asks visitors whether "they have decided they want what we have." In other words, do you see something here that is so compelling that you want to be a part of it?

LET IT SHINE

How would most visitors to your church answer that question?

Is there joy at your church? A sense of purpose? Fellowship and community? Hope? A sense of abundance?

Or is there fear? Consistent pessimism? Anger and infighting? Disengaged members who only seem to be there out of obligation?

Which of the two churches would you choose?

No church is perfect, nor is any Christian. But what a visitor sees on the surface of a church is a serious indication of that church's inner health. If newcomers see a church on life support that is not actively doing the work of getting well, they will not stay. Nor should they.

I have several very progressive friends who are raising their kids in conservative evangelical churches, often passing several progressive churches on their way each Sunday. They confess that they struggle with reconciling the Sunday sermon with the values they are trying to teach their kids at home. But when I ask them why they don't just go to a church more aligned with their values, I always get a variation of the same answer:

"We tried. We visited . . . but there was just nothing going on there."

I sometimes argue that something could be "going on there" if more families like theirs would just join. But the reality is that more conservative churches just do a few things better than more progressive churches. That is why they are so attractive, especially to younger families. It's not the music. It's not the gym with the rock-climbing wall. And it's not the new building.

It's the sense of purpose.

Generation X and millennial worshipers do not roam the suburbs in search of guitars and amplifiers. Instead, after growing up in a world where so much has been uncertain, and where so few of us have been exposed to rituals and traditions, we are looking for something rooted. Something substantial. Something that requires commitment from us.

That does not mean we want the easy answers or simplistic theologies that some churches offer. Quite the contrary. But the fact that so many are willing to put up with those things in order to find the other things we are seeking should say something to the progressive church.

It's especially crucial that we ask ourselves why we are failing, because if there ever was a time for a rise in progressive faith, it is now. But it won't happen until we figure some things out. Starting with ourselves.

It is my firm belief that church growth and church vitality are tied to one thing above all others: the quality of our discipleship.

And more than anything, I believe that discipleship is about the will to change and to be changed. It's about finding our purpose, and reordering our lives in order to pursue it. And it's about engaging in the work of transformation in ourselves before we try to do it in the world.

God is not done with us yet. Neither each of us as individuals, nor our churches or our denominations. Now is the time to do the work of becoming disciples. And our first step is to kick over the bushel basket, hold up the light, and let it shine.

3

Glory and Joy

WWJD?

When I started seminary in the late 1990s the question "What would Jesus do?" was all the rage. Woven bracelets with the acronym "WWJD" were worn by seemingly every church youth group member in good standing. And someone was making a mint off the T-shirt marketing.

"What would Jesus do?" was an interesting question. But to be honest, I never knew how to answer it. I could usually guess at it, but I never was quite sure how Jesus would act in any given situation. In the end the whole thing felt like easy ethics and half-hearted speculation to me.

"Be nice? Be kind? Try to smooth things over?"

It just didn't feel right. It was all a little too pat and easy and *kumbaya* for me.

Around the same time, a seminary professor of mine had a bumper sticker made that asked an alternative question: "DIGG?" or "Does it glorify God?"

Glory and Joy

It never exactly caught on. No DIGG posters were printed and hung in dorm rooms. But nonetheless, it intrigued me.

It's important to give a little context to the professor's question. While they may have come up with the acronym, they were far from the first to put supreme importance on the idea of glorifying God. That idea has been around, literally, for ages.

I went to a Presbyterian seminary, the kind that valued historic confessions of faith and catechisms. Our theology professors made sure its students were at least vaguely familiar with the Westminster Shorter Catechism, which at one time every good Presbyterian youth had memorized.

It's pretty easy to dismiss the Catechism, written by a group of theologians and English Parliament members called the Assembly of Divines during 1646–1647, as irrelevant to the church today. And I certainly would not advocate that my youth group spend time memorizing it, nor would I say that it is a flawless and complete guide to Christian faith. And yet, I still find some wisdom there, as did generations of Presbyterians and the Congregationalists who later became part of the UCC. It's a deep part of the theological heritage of these traditions, one we cannot simply throw out.

The best example of why I think this is within the first question the catechism asks (edited for inclusivity):

Question: What is the chief end of [humankind]?

Answer: [Humanity's] chief end is to glorify God, and to enjoy [God] forever.

In other words, "What's our purpose in life?"

"To give glory to God, and to live joyfully because of God."

It's still hard for me to think of the dour old Westminster Divines as a particularly joyful bunch, but apparently they saw it as important enough to put it right there at the start. But that joy did not exist by itself. It existed in tandem with this: the command to glorify God.

That gets me back to those wristbands and bumper stickers. I never knew how to answer the first question, "What would Jesus do?" But that second question? "Does it glorify God?" That's the one that got to me. And that's the one I started to ask myself more regularly.

Nearly four hundred years after the Westminster Shorter Catechism was written, I still think that first answer to the catechism is the best one-line synopsis of what it means to live a Christian life. In the end our choices should not be about what brings us glory. Instead, they should be about what glorifies God.

A side note here for those who are not a part of the Reformed tradition. The Reformed tradition is the theological movement that descends from the seventeenth-century work of John Calvin and his contemporaries. Over the course of nearly five hundred years that tradition has grown, transformed, and become increasingly diverse in every sense of the word.

The Presbyterian Church (USA) and the United Church of Christ are two historically Reformed traditions. They are also two of the most progressive of contemporary Reformed traditions. Many Reformed traditions do indeed renounce homosexuality, stick to a seven-day view of creation, and bar women from leadership roles.

But the Presbyterian and UCC traditions epitomize what I believe to be the true aim of the Reformed faith as captured by this well-known Reformed phrase: *Ecclesia reformata et semper reformanda secundum verbum Dei.* That is, "the church Reformed and always being reformed according to the Word of God." Put another way, to paraphrase the Rev. John Robinson as he sent off the Mayflower Pilgrims, "God has yet more light and truth to break forth from God's holy word." Or, to use the current catchphrase of the United Church of Christ, "God is still speaking."

The Westminster Catechism is a decidedly Reformed document. It is a product of both its tradition and its time, and it is not infallible. And yet, even if you are not Reformed, I believe that its exhortation to both "glorify" and "enjoy" God speaks to us today. I also believe that it speaks beyond denominational and traditional lines.

Just as I, as a liberal Reformed Christian, can find wisdom in John Wesley and Martin Luther, I believe other Christians can find something of value in the Reformed faith. Unfortunately, the denominational lines drawn hundreds of years ago in Europe still define the face of mainline American Protestantism to this day. But with mainline decline comes the need to break down these barriers in order to find renewal.

Though I love my own denomination, by the time I retire, I'm not so sure it will look anything like it does today. I believe either we will have merged with other, like-minded denominations or we will exist as a loose band of connected congregations. But whatever the future holds, I'm positive that a renewal of the mainline Protestantism, and our progressive Christian hopes for the world, is impossible if we remain in our denominational silos.

We need to find the things on which we can agree, and we need to build upon those points of common connection. We also need to share our own theological heritages with one another, and learn from them. That's why, though the language we use to describe it may be slightly different, I truly believe that the idea of finding greater purpose in glorifying God is one of many things that we can all agree upon.

GLORY

But what does it even mean to "glorify" God? The best way I know to answer that question is to point to one specific place in the worship service: the doxology. If you're like many mainline Protestants, you may associate the doxology with the short song that's sung when the collected offering is brought forward in the worship service, the one that starts, "Praise God from whom all blessings flow . . ."

When most churches take up the offering, the only thing that goes in the plates is money. We put in what we have to give, the plates are brought forward as the doxology is sung, and the pastor offers a prayer of dedication.

But the doxology isn't the "show me the money song." We don't sing it to say, "Look at all the checks we have for you, God." And it's not the musical cover that lets the ushers get to the front of the sanctuary.

The doxology makes sense following the call to the offering and the collection, though. As much as we associate stewardship solely with the financial, stewardship is about so much more than that. Stewardship is the process of saying, "This is what I have, and this is how I'm going to use it in this world."

When we are asked to give our offerings at church, we are called to take stock of everything we have received from God. We then make a conscious decision to dedicate what we have been given to the service of God and God's people. We need to find a better way in the church to make it clear that we are not just talking about money here (though we can't dismiss this aspect either).

Instead, ideally we bring to God the offering of our whole lives. Truly none of us can do this completely or perfectly. But when the call to the offering comes on Sundays, my hope is that— at least in our hearts, and at least in the moment—we are moved by the desire to want to give our very being to God.

When I bless the offering each week at church, I ask God to bless the congregation with wisdom to know how to use well all that has been brought forward. But then I offer another prayers. I ask that God would bless each of us that we would be offerings to God, and also God's offerings to the world. I ask that God would use us to bring light, grace, and peace to a world that needs all of those things so badly.

And what I am really saying is this: Help us to glorify you, God.

The root of the word "doxology" itself comes from two ancient Greek words: *doxa* and *logos*. The first word, *doxa*, means "glory" or "praise," especially of what is good. And the second, *logos*, means "words." So the doxology literally means "words of glory."

It's no coincidence that we sing about glorifying God at the offering. In a well-structured worship service the offering will come after we as the people of God have gathered together and heard the word proclaimed in both the reading of Scripture and the preaching of the sermon.

And now, having hopefully been changed or reached or moved in at least some small way, we are asked to respond to the Word. The offering is the opportunity to recommit oneself to doing the work of God's people in the world. The focal point is not the passed plate and what is placed in it. But the plate itself can be a metaphor for the larger response we are being asked to give. It is a symbol of whether or not we are "all in" and ready to do this work.

So when the plates are brought forward, the important question is not whether or not your offering envelope made it in this week. It's whether or not you have committed to make the offering of yourself and your heart, hands, and head. It's about whether or not you have decided you want to glorify God with your life.

And yet, we often stand and sing that familiar "Old Hundredth" hymn, whichever particular words we use, disconnected from its deeper meaning. At my church the doxology comes just before the final hymn and the benediction. It's the cue that the service is almost over.

But that's when those words matter more than ever, because that's when we are being sent into the world to do the work of the people of God. That's when we walk out the doors and make a choice about whether or not our actions on any given week will glorify God. That's when we need to be singing that doxology with conviction, not just as a commitment, but as a prayer to God for strength and for wisdom and, above all, for a reminder of our purpose.

WHY ARE YOU HERE?

We do not glorify God because God needs our glory. And we do not do it because God needs fame. God is a not a celebrity, in need of good publicists; though, frankly, God could use some new ones.

I believe we glorify God because that is what we were made to do. This is our default mode. The Westminster Catechism speaks of our "chief end," which is just 1640s language for this: What is our purpose? Or, why are we here?

And purpose is what the progressive Christian tradition needs.

That's not to say that we aren't getting things done. Sure, we are busy. There's the pride parade on Saturday, the peace rally on Tuesday, and the protest at city hall on Thursday. We have actions and obligations galore.

But do we have a sense of purpose?

No one can argue that justice, equality, and peace are not admirable purposes. But, for Christians, the pursuit of these things is rooted in something much deeper, something that makes it our obligation to work for them. That something renews us so that we can continue this work for the long term.

This purpose should drive Christians both as individuals and as communities. It should help people to find meaning in their own lives, and it should bind congregations and denominations together behind holy work.

But so often our good works are often done with only obligatory lip service to God. We are well-intentioned in our desire to tie them to our faith, but somewhere down the line God seems to get lost in the mix. And in the mixed company of social justice gatherings, we may even find ourselves being a little shy and apologetic about mentioning our faith.

All the while progressive churches in particular seem to cultivate a sort of revolving door of burned-out members. Visitors overjoyed by finding our churches, with their inclusive welcome and emphasis on social action, are often quick to commit. And, in our often numerically declining congregations, we are quick to let them.

New members become deacons or trustees. They work hard in our food pantries. They are there for every march or social action. They become pillars of the church. But too often, after a year or two, many of these new members stop appearing.

It may be because of a minor church conflict. Or it may be that something else comes up in their lives. There may be a million other reasons. But in many cases we need to call it what it is: burnout.

That word "burnout" perfectly describes the spiritual phenomenon of what happens to too many who walk through our doors. Think of the last campfire or bonfire you saw. When new wood is added to a fire that is already burning strongly, it becomes consumed but burns slowly, adding to the warmth and light for hours.

But what happens when good wood is thrown on top of a smoldering fire?

If you are lucky, or if you drench it in lighter fluid, it catches fire quickly and provides bright light. But without anything there to support it, without kindling or oxygen, it will burn fast and bright and then extinguish itself.

Too many of our congregations are like smoldering fires just waiting for new wood in the hopes that it will reignite us. New members come and give us hope for a little while, but more often than not, they don't stick around.

I truly believe that is because we in the progressive churches often fail to create a culture of discipleship. Our more conservative Christian siblings may not always lead the charge on social justice issues, but they know how to disciple, or teach, people. Whether someone is walking into a church for the first time in their lives, coming back after years away, or has been in the pews every Sunday since childhood, there is an emphasis on helping that person to grow spiritually.

And spiritual growth starts with knowing your purpose, and knowing who and whose you are. A church culture that encourages this growth acts like oxygen to a fire. The flames are fed, and the fire blazes. But a church culture that dismisses faith development and spiritual growth, and that fails to cultivate a sense of purpose, acts like a natural damper. The fire will burn out, one log at a time, until all you have left are ashes.

JOY

I often hear of people who leave their church because they are not "being fed."

Clergy friends of mine are quick to scoff at this. "Church is not about you, and your entertainment," they say. And that's very true. If your problem with your church is that your pastor's sermons are a little too dry, or the music isn't exactly what you'd prefer, that's a pretty flimsy reason for leaving.

But if the problem is that you are not being spiritually fed, that's a different issue altogether. I always tell those wishing to leave their church to see if they can help to transform the culture first. However, if there is little to no will to change, we have no right to expect members to stay in churches that are not equipping them to live lives of faith and purpose. I'll say more on this later, but for now I'll leave it at this: we can't hold people hostage who could get what they spiritually need elsewhere.

One of the greatest indicators I believe churches have about whether or not they are doing the work of cultivating a sense of purpose in their congregations and feeding the spiritually hungry is this: joy.

Have you ever walked into a church and immediately felt a palpable lack of joy? I've visited churches where the moment I walked through the sanctuary doors and was handed a bulletin by a dour usher I wanted to run. Church growth experts tell us that people decide whether or not to return to a church within anywhere from the first five to ten minutes after they walk through the doors.

While experts disagree on just how long it takes, one thing is clear: for all the pressure we put on clergy to be engaging, if you haven't conveyed something positive to your visitors long before your pastor starts preaching, they are most likely never coming back. And nothing turns people off faster than a lack of sincere welcome, and a lack of a sense of palpable joy.

Joy does not always come easily to those of us in the "frozen chosen" traditions. We prefer quiet dignity and reserved praise. On another level, for those of us who are so keenly aware of the inequalities and pain of the world, being asked to be joyful may even be met with suspicion. How can we be joyful when so many suffer?

The Apostle Paul told the Philippians to "rejoice in the Lord always; again I will say, rejoice." He could be saying the same thing to our churches today, churches that are often filled with negativity and a sense of despair, both for ourselves and for the world.

So, there is a question for us to ask ourselves as individuals, and also one every church should periodically ask itself: With all the choices people can make with what to do with their time and resources these days, who would want to be a part of something negative? How much more attractive are we when we are positive? And how much more powerful is our witness to Christ when we rejoice?

Right about now you might be thinking, well, that's all well and good, but it's naive. I mean, someone has to play devil's advocate. Someone needs to think of the worst-case scenario. Someone has to snap us back into reality. You preacher types like Paul, you just don't get the way the real world works.

Except Paul did get it. He got it more than we realize. When Paul wrote this letter, this exhortation to a church to "rejoice" and lift up what is good, how do you picture him? At a comfortable desk somewhere? Sitting down with a five-year plan that spelled out everything that was about to happen with great confidence and excitement? Relaxing?

Those are fair assumptions. It's pretty easy to say "rejoice" when things are going well for you.

But that's not what was going on. When Paul wrote this letter about joy, he was in prison, and he was waiting for his sentencing. He knew he was literally facing losing his life. Nothing was good or comfortable or happy.

And yet, he was full of joy. How can that be?

Here's what I think. I think it's easy to be joyless in this world. It's simple. It doesn't take much effort. You can put others down. You can dwell in hopelessness. You can even lob out negative reviews on the Internet from the comfort of your own home. The best part is that if you lack joy, you don't even have to do anything constructive. You can just dwell in it.

But it is a whole lot harder to rejoice. Why? Because joy is hard.

Now that may sound like an oxymoron. Joy is joy. Shouldn't joy be easy?

I don't think so. Because I think joy is deeper than that. Joy and happiness are two different things. Happiness is easy, but it's fleeting. You can find happiness in everything from a stiff drink to a big paycheck, from a nice meal to a new car. You can get happy pretty easily, at least for a little while. And then you can lose it just as quickly.

In comparison, joy is hard. But it's also deep. It's rooted. And it's the thing that remains in you even when everything else around you is crumbling down. Joy was there that day with Paul in that prison cell, and it wasn't an accident. It was there because Paul had a concrete sense of purpose.

Paul knew his purpose in life, and so he had carefully chosen the places where he would put his trust and his faith, and they weren't in the fleeting things of this world. They weren't in the things we can hold on to or lose. They were solely in this: God's love, and Christ's grace. Paul's sense of purpose transformed his life, even in the darkest of times. Even when everything else in the world was taken away from him, no one could touch his joy. And so, when Paul tells us to rejoice, I think he knows what he is talking about.

WOULD YOU CHANGE?

But if we are going to be like Paul, and be people of profound joy, we are going to have to change.

The folk musician Tracy Chapman sings a song in which she asks a series of questions. "If you saw the face of God and love," she sings at one point, "would you change?" At another she asks the listener what it would take to change: "How bad, how good does it need to get? How many losses, how much regret?"[2]

Whenever I hear that song, I can't help but think of the church. That's because sometimes I wonder what could force us to make the changes we need to make in order to be renewed. That's also because I know that if there is one thing the institutional church fears the most, it is change.

But what if you knew it could be better?

I have spent a lot of time around recovery communities, the sort that people come to only when they have hit "rock bottom." And I've come to think of rock bottom as a kind of gift from God. J. K. Rowling, the author of the Harry Potter series, describes the hardest period of her life this way: "Rock bottom became the solid foundation on which I built my life."[3]

I think rock bottom is such a powerful place to land because it is the one place where you are faced with a clear choice: get well, or die.

It's always heartbreaking to me how many choose the latter. But it's not surprising. Because the work of recovery is not easy, and it demands that the participant change their whole life. And, more than anything, recovery means they have to figure out their purpose in life, and make it their "solid foundation."

We progressive Christians have been hearing for decades that the mainline church is dying. I don't think we're there yet, but I do think we've hit rock bottom in a lot of ways. And I do think that we can make two choices at this point: choose to do nothing new, and die. Or choose to change, and recover.

If we choose life, we must also choose purpose. And if we believe our purpose truly comes from glorifying God, then we must work with God to change our lives and our churches. I truly believe recommitting to this purpose will only bring joy to the people of God. And I believe that those people of joy and purpose have the best chance of truly changing this world for the better.

In the next two sections of this book, change is going to take center stage. We're going to be talking about transformation. First, in part 2, we will look at what it means to be transformed into disciples. And then, in part 3, we will look at what it means to be transformative witnesses to God's love in the world.

If you are not willing to talk about change, stop reading now. The rest of the book will be a waste of time. But if you believe that with God we can change, and that God can indeed use us for a greater purpose, then read on.

PART TWO

BEING TRANSFORMED BY GOD

4

DISCIPLESHIP AS TRANSFORMATION

WHY ARE YOU HERE?

During my first year serving at my current church I preached a sermon series called "Why are we here?"

Though it sounded like the sort of existential question you'd be asked in a freshman philosophy class, that's not how I meant it. It wasn't about the big, existential questions like why are you alive, or why are you here on earth, or why does any of this exist. I meant in a very simple sense: why are you here at church this morning?

After all, I told them, you do have other options. You could be home, sleeping in. You could be out running errands at the grocery store or doing home repairs. You could be sipping coffee and eating eggs benedict. Brunch is a wonderful thing, you know. You could be in so many places right now other than sitting in the hard pews at church on a weekend. And yet, you are here. Why?

Everyone will answer that question differently, of course, but when I have really asked people to think about that question, and when they've taken some time and then told me about their thoughts, at the core of nearly every answer is this: a sense that God has something more in store for us.

We've already talked about purpose, and about glorifying God. But what does that mean in practice? And how do we become the sort of people who routinely do that?

I believe the work of Christians, and of the churches in which they are gathered, is to become two things: disciples and witnesses. And I also believe that there is something of an order to that process. In order to be witnesses to God's love in the world, I believe we first have to learn to be Christ's disciples.

The problem is that progressive churches often skip the discipleship phase and go right to acting as witnesses. That's not surprising. We are people who like to get stuff done. Why sit around and talk about our faith when we can be out acting on it? Who needs to read Scripture when there are Habitat for Humanity houses to be built?

In a practical sense, no one. In fact, you don't need worship to do that either. You don't even need to be a Christian or a person of faith. You can be completely devoid of any spiritual conviction whatsoever and still do good works in this world.

In fact, if the goal is the production of tangible results, it might even be more efficient to just remove church completely from the picture. There are certainly nonprofits out there that do a far better job than we do.

But if we believe that being a Christian is about more than just works, and if we believe that who we are as children of God matters, then we have to start by grounding our actions and identity in something greater than ourselves. That's the work of discipleship. And that work, that growth, means we must be ready to learn and to be changed.

TO LEARN

Listen! A sower went out to sow. . . . Other seeds fell on rocky ground, where they did not have much soil, and they sprang up quickly, since they had no depth of soil. But when the sun rose, they were scorched; and since they had no root, they withered away. . . . Other seeds fell on good soil and brought forth grain, some a hundredfold, some sixty, some thirty. Let anyone with ears listen! (Matt. 13)

Jesus is talking about seeds in the parable of the sower, but really I think he is talking about discipleship and all of us. If we are seeds scattered on the ground, full of the potential to grow and flourish, where we are planted matters. If the ground we are planted in is not deep, and the soil dry, we will bloom quickly and then just fade away. But if we find good soil and become deeply rooted in it, we will grow abundantly.

Without cultivating discipleship, we as Christians are unrooted. But when we value discipleship and commit to the lifelong journey of faith, we put down roots in good soil.

First, what is a disciple, anyway? We hear that word and we might think it's limited to the twelve guys who always followed Jesus around. Yet the reality is that disciples transcend the ages, and the calling to be a disciple is open to all of us.

Take a minute and think about how you understand that word "disciple."

When you hear it do you automatically think "follower of Jesus"? That wouldn't be surprising. The word has certainly come to take on that meaning. But the reality is that the word has been used for many other followers too. In Jesus' time a lot of teachers and leaders had a group of disciples. Even John the Baptist, who was loyal to Jesus from the beginning, had his own, and they followed him just like the disciples who followed Jesus.

Disciples would follow someone attentively because being a disciple, to anyone, had to do with one thing in particular: learning. Disciples sincerely thought that the person they were following had something to teach. So much so that the actual word used for "disciples" in the original New Testament texts, written in Greek, is *mathetes*. You don't need to remember that exact word, but know that the easiest translation of it is simply this: students, or learners.

That's an easy sell in my context. The church I serve is right next to a well-known boarding school, and we are located in an area where education is given top priority. Many of my parishioners are teachers or educators of some kind. They also want well-educated church leaders. And I would guess that if I asked any of them what they wanted for their children or grandchildren or any other young person in their lives, one of the first things they would say would be "I want them to get a good education." Or "I want them to love learning."

That's a good thing because you can't help but grow when you learn. Conversely, when you stop learning, you stop growing.

The same is true for Christians. If we stop learning and growing, then we can't do any of the work of the church. Learning is the way we prepare to be Christians. But even in churches that are filled with highly educated people, we sometimes forget that.

Just think of two words we often use interchangeably, especially in regards to the twelve Jesus first called: "disciple" and "apostle." Despite our usage, those two words don't mean the same thing. "Disciple" means "student," but "apostle" means "messenger" or one who is "sent out."

The Bible doesn't use the word "apostle" for the twelve until later on, because before Jesus set his disciples loose on the world to be his messengers, he first had to teach them. They had to follow him, ask questions, and see how he lived. Only after they had been disciples, students of Jesus and his life, could they become the teachers themselves.

Jesus didn't call them out of the boats and say, "Now you are fishers of people," after all. He called them and said, "I will make you fishers of people."

But in order to become disciples, simply reading and listening is not enough. One can devote hours to the academic study of Christian faith without any real desire to be a disciple. In order to be that, you have to take it one step further; you have to be willing to grow. And there is no growth I know of that does not demand change.

TO BE CHANGED

There is a story in Scripture about a man who comes to Jesus with what the text calls an "unclean spirit," or a demon. He's agitated and yelling and calling out to Jesus, asking if Jesus has come to destroy the demons. It should be noted that the man does not seem excited about that possibility.

Jesus says to the demons, "Be quiet, and come out of him." And they do.

That's when everyone gets really scared. Because not only does Jesus teach like he has authority, but he can do things and create changes that no one has ever seen before. And change, real change, is scary. It's not just the inconvenience of your daily routine being switched up a little. It's the kind of change that takes everything you have known about yourself and who you are and shakes it up forever.

Jesus was all about change. He changed everyone's understanding of what it meant to worship God. He changed people's actual lives, like the man he healed in the synagogue. He changed everything.

But, more than that, Jesus was the change. Everything about Jesus and his life means that nothing about us or our lives is safe from change.

Because of that, this is what I believe: following Jesus, being his disciple, is not safe. It is not comfortable. And it is not something you can do if you really just want everything to be the same as it has always been. Being a follower of Jesus means that you and your life are going to be changed, and sometimes that change is not going to be all that convenient.

Scripture doesn't tell us what happened to that man Jesus healed that day. All we really know is he had been changed in a profound way for the better. But in that moment and the ones that followed, do you think he was scared? Do you think that for just a moment he wished that he had never met Jesus? Do you think that he almost wished he could go back to the life he knew, the one where he had learned to live with his demons?

I think he probably did. I say that because all of us have had our demons. I don't mean that in the actual literal sense, but in a metaphorical but still all-too-real sense. All of us have had our battles, and our moments of having to fight them. And all of us, if we have made a decision to overcome those demons, have had to say, "I'm ready to be changed, no matter the cost."

If you've ever done that, my guess is you've also had a moment where you've said, "Is all this really worth it? Were things really all that bad before?" And maybe you've wished, for just a second, that you had never believed change was possible.

That makes sense, because change is never easy. But the good news is that the same Jesus who is all about change is also all about new life. Sometimes we just need to let God change us in order to get us there.

That means, first, each of us must be changed individually. That's because a big part of the Christian life is about being transformed by the fact that you are a follower of Jesus Christ. That word "follower" is more important than it may sound. Because to be a follower of Christ, you have to actually follow. You can't just stand still. You have to be willing to move with Christ.

When you are moving with Christ and following him, you cannot help but be transformed by who he is. You cannot help but be changed. Sometimes that is going to be wonderful, and sometimes it is going to be staggeringly inconvenient and difficult. And it's going to happen again and again and again.

Even when you think, "I've reached the summit . . . there's nothing more God can do with me," that's when you are going to be changed again. But the good news is that if that transformation really is about, and comes from, God, then it is always going to be life giving. It can't help but be. So when we look back, we will see that God has only changed us for the better, and that God has never failed to give us new life once again.

GRACE

But really, are things that bad? Do we really need to change? Do we really have so much to learn?

I can't answer for you, but I believe most of us can acknowledge that we are not perfect. We make mistakes. We make the wrong things our priorities. We are silent when we could speak out. And we hurt the people we love, even when we don't want to.

This is called sin.

Are you uncomfortable right now? I'd be surprised if you weren't, because I'm uncomfortable writing it. Experience tells me this is not sitting well with at least some of you right now.

I was once giving a series of lectures to a wonderfully engaged group. It was clear that what I was saying was resonating as heads nodded and notes were taken. And then one day I talked about sin, and the mood changed.

"It's so negative."

"Can't we use another word for it?"

"Saying that people sin sounds so, well, judgmental."

No one likes to talk about sin. Especially in the progressive church. We talk instead about making a mistake, or the wrong life choices. But we get squeamish when we are asked to call something sinful, even if it's our own action.

I get why. Judgmental Christians have given us all a bad name. But on the other hand, there is a freedom in being able to admit that sometimes we are imperfect, sometimes we fall short, and sometimes we do not act the way God would have us act.

The greatest theological work of our time, which is of course the Harry Potter series, taught us that "fear of the name only increases fear of the thing itself." Sure, Hermione was talking about Voldemort there, but the same thing applies to sin. If we get too afraid to even speak its name, it holds a certain fearful power over us.

And so, I say this freely: I'm a sinner. And so are you. And so are we all. Because none of us is perfect, and none of us always gets it right. In the end sin is just shorthand for saying that sometimes our will and actions are not in full alignment with God's. If we cannot admit that truth, we cannot do the work of discipleship.

But, by the grace of God, most of us are capable of being honest with ourselves, and most of us have the will to want to learn and change. And I say "by the grace of God" because I truly believe it is only by God's grace that we are able to see the ways that both we and the world have far to go.

Reformed Christians love to talk about grace. All Christians do, really, but those of us who are Reformed in particular seem to be bitten extra hard by the grace bug. For me, the Reformed understanding of grace is one of the most beautiful, awesome, inspiring, and humbling things I have ever encountered.

The New Testament word for grace is *charis*. It can also be translated as "kindness" or "favor." Sometimes it is even translated as "a gift." That's because grace, first and foremost, is not something that we earn, nor something we work to receive. That, by very definition, is not grace.

Instead, grace is what God gives to us solely because God loves us, and not because we have done anything to deserve it. Grace is God's continued involvement in our life and God's life-saving and life-giving guidance and intervention, even when we make the worst possible choices.

In the South, where I grew up, many of my friends belonged to churches that taught that people would either be "saved" or "damned" by their own actions. Anything from not going to church to loving the "wrong" person meant an eternal sentence to a lake of fire. One could repent, of course, but "backsliders" were treated with suspicion and disdain.

After growing up with hell-inspired nightmares, the theology I learned in the Presbyterian Church was a relief. There I was taught that God's love for us is real and complete, and that God's grace is saving in and of itself. There was nothing I could do that would remove me from God's love. And, by extension, there was nothing I could do that would either earn me, or preclude me from, salvation.

Some conservative Reformed Christians take this to an extreme and believe in something called "double-predestination." That is, God chooses some of us for heaven, and some for hell. But for most of the more moderate and progressive Reformed Christians out there, grace just means that God's love is so big that none of us will be forgotten or cast aside. God will continue to actively love us and to transform us.

It is grace, then, that helps us to see that we can do better. In fact, it is grace that shows us that God wants better for us.

This is true for us as individuals, but it is also true of larger groups, because sin can be systemic as well. And systems of sin are even harder to change than the hearts of individuals. One only needs to look at the world to see the ways that systemic sin manifests itself: racism, poverty, sexism, environmental destruction, homophobia, war, transphobia, sexual violence, and more. These all thrive because they are built upon a structure of systemic sin.

To dismantle these structures will take the work of committed individuals who will look for God's grace and the guidance of the Holy Spirit that comes with it. But before we can even begin to focus on fixing the world outside of our doors, we first need to be willing to take an honest look at ourselves. We cannot save the world if we are unwilling to do the hard work of telling the truth about ourselves, and committing to the work of becoming disciples. This is crucial because discipleship is about knowingly needing and responding to the grace of God.

COMING HOME

Telling the truth is the work of the gospel, and the work of the church. John's Gospel tells us, "and you shall know the truth, and the truth shall set you free." That is a radically countercultural idea today because, as much as we are a culture of oversharing and overexposure, we are not a culture of truth telling.

For that reason, as hard as it is, we should want churches that will tell us the truth. We should want churches that can speak the truth about our own imperfections, and our need for God's grace. And we should want churches that will challenge us to respond to God's grace not by dwelling in shame and guilt, but instead by committing to personal transformation.

One word we use for this is "repentance." That word might evoke negative images for some, like the fundamentalist preacher who yells at the congregation saying, "Repent, sinners!" or the penitents who wait patiently to tell a priest their darkest sins.

But at its root, repentance is simply this: to return to right relationship with God. The Hebrew word closest to the English word "repentance" is *teshuvah*, or "to turn back." The Greek word from the New Testament that has traditionally been translated as repentance is *metanoia*. A better translation, though, would be "to change one's mind." In other words, to repent, in a biblical sense, is to change one's thinking and turn back towards God, by the grace of God.

Repentance is about repairing a relationship, in this case our relationship with God. It's about telling the truth about what we have done, and finding only love and forgiveness in the arms of the Creator. It's about coming home.

We return home by deciding our faith in a loving God will not be peripheral to the rest of our life. Instead, it will be the lens through which we view ourselves and the world. That's not always easy, because relationships never are; but they can also be the most rewarding parts of our life.

You probably know what it's like to be in relationship with God because you know what it's like to be in relationship with another, whether friend or partner or family member. You know what it's like to care enough about someone to know that your choices affect them, and you know that the relationship doesn't work if it stays peripheral. It only works when it stays honest and centered.

It's the same way with God. God never chooses to leave us, but we sometimes do things that make ourselves drift away from God. Because of that, too often we find ourselves off alone on a path of our own creation, instead of with the God who loves us more than we know.

That's when we can repent and when we can look at what feels disjointed or disconnected in our lives. That's when we can say to God, I'm tired of walking alone. I want to come back and walk with you. I want to come home.

NEVER THE SAME AGAIN

Homecoming is a form of resurrection. That's fitting because Christians are Easter people. It's not clear who first used the phrase "Easter people" to describe us, but they were absolutely right. We follow Christ knowing that the love of God will have the final say, and that not even death will be able to triumph over life.

But, as many others have pointed out, we far too often live in a "Good Friday world," full of all the pain that systemic sin can bring. We are living in an era where war drives refugees across borders into unwelcoming arms. One where we have the capacity to feed every child of God but simply choose not to do so. And, perhaps most disturbingly, we are living in a time when humanity itself is rapidly destroying our own home through environmental recklessness.

And yet, we remain Easter people. Resurrection is not just about what happened to Christ two thousand years ago. It's about what is happening to the people of God each and every day. Our own transformations become our resurrections.

That's both wonderful, and staggeringly inconvenient. Wonderful because new life is always wonderful. But inconvenient because once we know there is a better way, once we know that resurrection and new life are possible, we can never settle for the Good Friday world again.

Recently I read a book by John Lewis, the congressman from Georgia who was intimately involved in the civil rights movement. In it he told a story that was about his own transformation. When he was in early high school in a segregated school in rural Alabama, one with few resources, his uncle took him to New York state for the summer. That summer, for the first time in his life, he saw blacks and whites living, working, shopping, and eating side by side. He saw educational opportunities that he didn't know were there for him. He saw a future he had never imagined in rural Alabama.

At the end of the summer, he had to go back home to the South, and back to where he was treated as less than equal. And for the first time he really understood what segregation was all about. It must have felt like going back in time. But it was the experience of going and seeing another way, and then coming back and knowing that things could be different, that John Lewis credits with giving him the desire to push for change. It was the catalyst for all he would later do in his life.

I tell you this story not because John Lewis or anyone else who lived under the sin of segregation was in any way responsible for that. I tell it because it's a powerful example of how sometimes once we see what is possible we are never the same again, and once we see that new life is possible we cannot help but try to change our own lives. We have to do the hard things. We have to decide what fears we won't let control our lives anymore, and then we have to make that same decision again and again, day after day. Somewhere in that process, we become resurrection people.

That's how you know you are becoming a disciple. You know you have learned and changed because, even when you stumble, the grace of God shows you that there's a better way. That same grace gives you no choice but to stand back up and keep moving forward, and to keep moving towards home.

5

WHAT BINDS US TOGETHER

BOWLING ALONE

In 2000 the political scientist Robert Putnam published a book about his observations on the decline of social involvement in the United States. *Bowling Alone: The Collapse and Revival of American Community* made quite a splash among not just academics, but also those who care about participatory democracy and community building.

On his website bowlingalone.com, Putnam says the book "draws on evidence including nearly 500,000 interviews over the last quarter century to show that we sign fewer petitions, belong to fewer organizations that meet, know our neighbors less, meet with friends less frequently, and even socialize with our families less often. We're even bowling alone. More Americans are bowling than ever before, but they are not bowling in leagues."

The metaphor of bowling is woven through the book. Bowling leagues, once abundant in America, are nearing extinction. Putnam writes, "Between 1980 and 1993 the total number of bowlers in America increased by 10 percent, while league bowling decreased by more than 40 percent."[4] In other words, even as the sport grows, more and more people are "bowling alone."

But this isn't just about bowling. Putnam points out the steady decline in institutions that have traditionally been strong. From their peak years until 1997, these groups all declined in membership: Freemasons (–71 percent), the American Legion (–47 percent), Red Cross volunteers (–61 percent), the PTA (–60 percent), Rotary (–25 percent), and the General Federation of Women's Clubs (–84 percent).[5]

In other words, we have become a nation of nonjoiners and unjoiners —either never joining or discontinuing membership in groups—rapidly becoming less connected with one another via formal means.

So, you could be saying, that's not a big deal. The time of fraternal and social groups has passed, and perhaps the "joining" model has seen its day. If you could also argue that our social connections to one another had somehow improved at the same time, I might agree with you. But they haven't.

Putnam found that over the past twenty-five years before the book's publication family dinners dropped by 43 percent and having friends over to our houses dropped by 35 percent. We are not trading club meetings for quality time with family and friends. In fact, what Putnam calls "social capital," which he defines as "not just warm and cuddly feelings, but a wide variety of quite specific benefits that flow from the trust, reciprocity, information, and cooperation associated with social networks," has plummeted.

In other words, when we are socially engaged we are "better together." Putnam even named his second book just that. But when we are not, we are in danger of losing social cohesion.

Fifteen years after the publication of *Bowling Alone* the world has changed. Social engagement has changed as well. In 2010 Putnam revisited his book along with Thomas Sander and found that in the post–9/11, social media–fueled world, civic engagement was indeed increasing . . .

in some ways. For instance, the number of college freshmen who talked to their classmates about politics was at an all-time high.[6]

But at the same time, formal joining continues to decline. Additionally, the socioeconomic gap between "haves" and "have nots," Putnam finds, has led to two very different Americas, with different levels of engagement. Trust rates have also declined, from more than 50 percent of people in the 1960s to less than a third today saying they "trust others." Even close friendships, the authors found, have declined precipitously.[7]

In other words, while the post–9/11 world may be more politically engaged (and, I would argue, divided) we are still "bowling alone." And though I am a staunch supporter of social media, and I believe it can be a marvelous tool for churches, we are not once again becoming a nation of joiners, no matter how many Facebook friends or Twitter followers we have.

RELIGION-ING ALONE

We are "religion-ing" alone, too. That's actually an oxymoron, and I'll get into why later, but the fact remains that even in faith we are more and more individualistic. *Bowling Alone* shows us that the joining problems that churches are seeing are far from isolated. Church decline is in a very real way associated with social disengagement as a whole.

The rise of the "nones" and of the "spiritual but not religious" folks bears out Putnam's premise. Spirituality, even when wrapped in something as seemingly disconnected as exercise, sells. Just look at yoga studios. So does soul searching and meaning making. Think of therapists who urge us to be our best selves. We are a people searching for self-actualization and spiritual perfection. And we are doing it alone.

There are plenty of voices out there telling you that you can connect with God on a hike, or over brunch, or at a party with a bunch of friends. I'm not saying that any of those things are false, but I am saying that I don't think they are enough. Because at the end of the day, the solitary spiritual life is just that: solitary. And I don't think God calls us out only to leave us alone.

The idea of social connection did not start with Putnam or any other contemporary figure. It's been alive far longer than that, and it was actively embraced by Jesus Christ. In the Gospel of John, Jesus begins to call his disciples. He goes to a man named Philip and calls to him saying, "Follow me." Philip does. And then Philip goes to his friend Nathaniel, and he tells him all about Jesus, and even though Nathaniel doesn't quite believe it, Philip tells him, "Come and see." Nathaniel does, and he finds out that everything Philip said was true.

When Christ called Philip, he didn't leave him alone for long. Right away Nathaniel joined the same journey, and then more and more disciples joined. The church is here today because Christ knew we are better together, and for generations we Christians have discovered the same thing. Chances are if you are a part of a church, there's something about that idea that appeals to you enough to keep you there.

That doesn't mean that you are no longer an individual. Each of us has come to the church on our own journey, our roads now converging together. As members of these communities we call church, we choose to bind part of our journey together. That's why I am here. That's why you are here. That's why each of us is here.

That's also what religion is all about. But religion often gets a bad rap.

You can hear that in the voices of the people who tell you they are "spiritual but not religious." Spirituality is good and pure, untouched by the constraints and failures of human organizations (or maybe even humans themselves). Religions, I've often been told, kill people. We start wars. We oppress women and LGBTQ folks. We turn our heads away from the evils of the world.

And that's true. Religious people have messed up big time throughout history, and they have often used radical misunderstandings of their own faiths in order to justify it. So have nonreligious people, by the way, but we're not talking about them here. We have to face up to the fact that we have sins for which we must atone.

While we do this work, though, we have to also find what is good in religion. When we do, we can see religion not as a hindrance to the spiritual life, but as a cultivator of it at its deepest levels.

If you look at one possible root of the word "religion," you may discover something I consider to be beautiful. The Latin word *religare* means "to tie" or "to bind." Religion is what ties us together and binds us into communities. It also gives structure to our lives, and acts as the connective tissue between belief and body.

There are, of course, major religions. Christianity, Islam, Judaism, Hinduism, and Buddhism, to name a few. And each of those faiths has its various movements and denominations. It would be a mistake, though, to think that these are the world's only religions.

The reality is that everyone has a religion, even those who claim only to be spiritual. That's true because each one of us, whether we admit it or not, has a system of beliefs or values that defines our life, for good or ill. Each of us is tied to either that which lifts us up or the baggage that pulls us down. In that sense we might do religion by ourselves, but we can never really do it alone.

Our religions are as varied as we are. We can worship in the church of career advancement, or the in the tabernacle of addiction. We can devote ourselves to running marathons, or make sacrifices on the altar of beauty. We can serve money as the ultimate god, or even devote our full faith to the idea that nothing exists beyond ourselves.

Religion is everywhere, and religion, at its most basic level, is simply a neutral concept. At its best our religion can make us better people, the kind who serve not just ourselves but the world. At its worst it can make us self-obsessed narcissists.

The communities we are a part of can often make a difference. They are the places where we are bound together with one another in the pursuit of our respective faiths. They are also the places where we are asked to do something quite countercultural: make a commitment.

REQUIRING SOMETHING OF US

There is a debate going on in clergy circles over whether or not we should move away from formal membership in the church. Jesus never required people to sign a membership roll, some reason, and people just aren't "joiners" anymore anyway. Putnam's research certainly bears that out.

And yet, community and commitment go hand in hand. Community, at its best, requires something from us. It is not just enough to be consumers, but in a society where consumer culture reigns supreme, that's a radical idea. Even the church has too often shaped itself around the needs of "church shoppers" and those who seek entertainment first on a Sunday morning.

We are often too careful about asking people to make a commitment for fear that we will scare them off. And so we trash the membership roll. We sheepishly hand out pledge cards telling people to fill one out if they feel like it. We tell the confirmation students that they can skip worship for Sunday morning soccer practice and still get confirmed.

But in doing away with all commitments, we begin to sever the ties that bind us to one another. The young and middle-aged adults who grew up in the commitment-free mainline churches of the '80s, '90s, and '00s are the "nones" of today. Their parents, whom we never managed to equip to be their children's greatest faith teachers, are the now empty nesters who are drifting away too. Their children are grown and their work, many figure, is done.

Meanwhile, commitment lives on in other organizations. Youth commit to being present for every elite team practice and game, lest they sit on the bench. The Marine Corps almost never fails to hit its recruiting goal, even in times of war. In a sort of reaction to the participation trophy culture they've grown up in, young people are seeking meaning through deeper commitments.

I believe that is because in a real way commitments make us clarify our priorities and our sense of identity. Recently I realized just how much so when I turned away an opportunity to join a local service club. Not only did membership in this club require attendance at weekly meetings, but members were expected to make up for weeks they missed by attending the meetings of neighboring clubs.

While I knew that my schedule would not allow me to be a faithful member, I have to admit I was impressed by the idea that membership required something. In an unintended way, the club's demands for my commitment forced me to clarify what really mattered to me. I decided my time would be better spent in other ways.

I think we are often reluctant to make similar requests for commitment in the church because we are afraid of rejection. If we ask for people to clarify their priorities, they just may discover that church is not one of them and leave for good. In an era when mainline churches are struggling to just get people in the doors, that terrifies us.

And yet, from the earliest days of the church, people have been asked to make commitments to the faith. When Jesus called the disciples, they literally dropped the fishing nets they were holding and walked away from everything to follow him. Many of those first disciples, and those they personally touched, would die for their faith.

In the twentieth century Lutheran theologian Dietrich Bonhoeffer reminded us of the demands of faith with the phrase "the cost of discipleship." "Cheap grace," he wrote, was when "the sacraments, the forgiveness of sin, and the consolations of religion are thrown away at cut prices . . . the account has been paid in advance; and, because it has been paid, everything can be had for nothing." Conversely, discipleship required something more of us. Bonhoeffer knew what he was talking about; he himself was martyred by the Nazis.

But for North American Christians, death and persecution are not even on the table. We are not being asked to sacrifice our lives for the faith. We aren't expected to do much of anything. And now we increasingly aren't even asked to make a commitment to a community.

That's too bad, because community requires the sort of commitment that has the power to reinvigorate faith. There's a reason Jesus never called his disciples and then left them alone. He called them into a community in which their commitment to the faith could be nourished, a community that managed to rise again even after every single one of them fled from Jesus in his hour of greatest need. It was the strength of the community, and not just the sum of the individuals, that helped the church to survive the persecution it was to face.

CAN YOU BAPTIZE MY BABY IN PRIVATE?

But will the church survive Sunday morning soccer practice?

Yes. Because the church is the eternal body of Christ. Will the mainline and progressive church survive, even in a radically different form? I wish I could say I was sure.

What I am sure about is that the actions we progressive Christians take now will do much to provide the final answer to that question. I'm also sure that one of the greatest indicators of a positive outcome will be whether or not we are able to build strong congregational communities full of committed disciples.

I think about that whenever I received a call from an unknown family asking me to baptize their baby. I'm always glad to welcome new families to the church, so I invite the parents to come in. But when I explain that baptisms are done, with only emergency exceptions, in the context of Sunday worship, more often than not I'm met with resistance.

"We were really hoping for a family-only ceremony," I'm told. Or "Since the church doesn't really know us, that would be awkward."

"This is a great chance to get to know the church," I tell them, "and to expand your family of faith."

Some parents choose to go elsewhere at this point, or else go nowhere at all. A few others stay long enough for the "splash and dash"; they attend church regularly until their child is baptized, and then we rarely ever see them again. But for others, bringing a child into a church community, and hearing the congregation make those baptismal promises to care for and nurture a child in the Christian faith, binds them to the local parish in a powerful way. In baptism the gathered church makes a commitment to a child who cannot commit anything back. That's a stunning witness to the beauty of community.

I want to show this community to couples who call me wanting to "rent the church" for weddings. "The sanctuary is not a picture-ready backdrop to your perfect day," I want to say, "and I am not a wedding vendor. This church is simply the physical home of a community of faith. If the big, white building were to fall tomorrow, the community that is gathered here would still be more beautiful than the most elaborate wedding celebration."

And I want to share it with the family and friends who always come up to pastors after funerals, as many of my colleagues and I have found, to tell us that "this may sound weird, that was the best funeral I have ever been to." I want to say to them, "That's not because I'm a great minister. That's because this church really knew your Aunt Betsy. She was here every week, in that pew, and she was there in the kitchen cooking for the church suppers, and she was there at Bible study on Wednesdays. She was known and loved in this place, and we miss her too."

That's the power of community. We know each person in an intimate way, and we are able to accompany them on their spiritual journey. Even when the human part of that journey is over, we are able to mourn one another and to say goodbye in a way that honors each as the unique child of God that they were, and to trust their soul to God in the next life.

This is in contrast to what often happens outside of the church doors where the rites of passage are more individualized and anonymous. Even the trend of parents wanting their children to be baptized privately shows this. Baptism becomes simply a ritual to check off a list, not a sign of entry into the community. The child receives the sacrament and then is expected to do the work of getting to know God on their own later in life.

But it's the community, gathered around Christ, where we are called to live into the sacrament. I often ask parents, "If you're not going to be active in a congregation, what's the point of baptism?" I assure them that their baby will not go to hell if it dies unbaptized, and that if this is truly about wanting their child to make "its own choices" about faith away from community, perhaps baptism should wait.

If the parents cannot make the baptismal promises to raise and nurture the child in the faith, then the reasons they want their child baptized make little sense in my congregation's Reformed context. I never deny a baptism to a family that truly wants one, but I do push them to clarify why they would want the sacrament enough to ask for it without being willing to then engage in a community that will sustain it. It is in those questions that the role of community often becomes more clear.

While society as a whole moves more towards a "bowling alone" culture, the church must choose a countercultural track. The ranks of the "nones" and "spiritual but not religious" may indeed grow, and that's okay. But the church should not be, as H. Richard Niebuhr might say, transformed by culture in this respect. Instead, we can instead seize this moment as a chance to counterculturally create disciples who have been transformed by Christ—disciples that we can then send out into a world that needs transformative community so desperately.

CHURCH IS WHO WE ARE

I write a weekly letter to the members and friends of my church. Every Friday morning it goes out via e-mail to their inboxes. And each week, I start it with the same salutation: Dear Church.

That sounded odd to some at first. Maybe even a bit impersonal. I could say "Dear members and friends of the Congregational Church in Exeter," for instance. But I believe that "Dear Church" is actually the most warm and personal greeting I can use.

That's because the church is who we are. Church is not a place we go or a group we join. It is the community that ties us together and strengthens us for the lives our faith in Christ calls us to lead. Each of us is the church. And, paradoxically, none of us can be the church alone.

Our church communities matter so much because they are the best manifestations of the body of Christ that we have in this life. As Christians we believe that the church is the living body of Christ, active and alive in the world. If you are going to follow Jesus Christ, the one who called his disciples into community, why would you not want to be a part of that body in some form?

The truth is, that has not always been easy for me personally. As a young Christian I wrestled with congregations. They always seemed to be messing things up and making mistakes. They were messy and frustrating. They seemed to be magnets for hard personalities and people on power trips. I truly believed that if Jesus came back the last place he'd be caught dead in was a church.

I left seminary and spent eight years as a chaplain and academic. Even when the work was fulfilling, though, I never felt like I was in the right place. I was running from the local church, and though I was an ordained minister, my faith life was beginning to feel like that of the "spiritual but not religious." I had never felt further from God in my life.

Things changed for me when I was able to acknowledge that church was indeed a frustrating, messy, difficult place filled with imperfect people. So was the first church that Jesus called to surround him. Jesus never planted himself in the midst of perfect people. He always chose works in progress, but he never chose them alone. I think he knew we'd need more than ourselves.

I have come to believe in the power of each congregation to transform lives and to then transform communities. One word we might use for this is *koinonia*, a biblical Greek word that translates to "fellowship" or "joint participation." It is a deeper sense of community, one centered around Christ. To create that kind of community is our calling as Christians.

In the end it is in this *koinonia*, in this Christian fellowship, where disciples and witnesses are built. It is in community where we become Christians, and remain Christians, even when faith is hard. And it is in community where we build commitments and exist for something greater than ourselves and our immediate circles. The congregation, the gathered community of individuals, is the basic unit of the Christian life. Without it, there is no hope of progressive renewal.

THE BEST WAY TO LEARN TO BE A CHRISTIAN

We must remember the focus on community, even as we prepare to turn our attention to cultivating the spiritual lives of individual Christians. In fact, without a community I would argue that no Christian's formation can ever fully begin. I think it is telling that just as Jesus called the disciples into community, he also made sure to tell his disciples to stay in that community with one another even after his death.

I was once listening to Dr. Mary Luti, a seminary professor known for her deep understanding of church history, give a lecture on the meaning of baptism and on how we learn to be followers of Christ. Despite her own deeply academic background, she didn't tell us to read more books, study harder, or attend more seminary classes. Instead she said this: Find someone whose Christian life you admire and study them.

I realized in that moment that this simple practice was exactly how I learned what it meant to be a Christian. It didn't matter how many degrees in theology I pursued. It mattered that I had people in my life who lived their daily lives in ways that glorified God.

I thought of a mentor of mine who in my twenties taught me to live in faith and not in fear. I thought about the way she talked about her own faith journey, and about how it shaped her priorities. And I thought about how even things that had seemed insignificant at the time, like the ways she showed up for me when I needed it, or the words she used when she prayed, had taught me powerful lessons about God.

I realized a simple truth: I am a follower of Jesus Christ, but I'm also following in the footsteps of a mighty cloud of witnesses who have walked these same roads. So are we all. Without the community surrounding us, and binding us to one another, we become lost so easily. But when others light the way for us, we find that the paths we can take to follow Christ are all around us, and we have multitude of willing companions on the journey.

6

ROOTED IN GOOD SOIL

CULTIVATING OUR SPIRITUAL SOIL

Last year a group of my colleagues and I led our congregations through a church growth exercise called Natural Church Development designed to determine our strengths and weaknesses. Each church had a number of members take a survey assessing the church's gifts and struggles. And before the results even came back, I knew that my church's growing edge would be what the survey described as "passionate spirituality."

I was right. The same was true of almost every one of my colleague's congregations as well. Not only did we all have the same lowest score in passionate spirituality, but I suspect the same would likely be true of the majority of mainline congregations as well. When it comes to our spiritual lives we are often not just lacking . . . we are downright suspect.

When we got our results back we shared them with our congregations, who gave us immediate feedback. "We don't want to be like *those* churches," they said. "We don't have a screen with a bouncing ball up front, or a rock band with drums and guitars. We don't raise our hands in church and shout 'Jesus.' Passionate spirituality is our lowest factor? Good!"

It's normal, after all, for human beings to justify why we have under-performed in something. We try to reason it away at first. But after a while, it became clear to my church that maybe the survey had been on to something.

Over time we learned that what the survey makers described as pas-sionate spirituality is not about the way you worship. You can find pas-sionate spirituality in mainline Protestant churches like ours, in Catholic churches with a formal liturgy, and even in quiet Quaker meetings.

It's also not about specific beliefs. You don't have to subscribe to a set view of God and sign on the dotted line. And it's not about being loud or flashy or being the next big thing.

Instead, it's about being passionate about your spiritual journey, the same way that you are passionate about the other things that matter in your life. It's also about being rooted in your relationship with the divine, and able to connect that to all that you do. If something is important to you, after all, it should give you life.

My spiritual connection with God is my guiding force in life. It helps me when I'm asked to make big decisions. It is always with me, and it is because of my faith that I live the way I do and make the choices I do on a daily basis.

Likewise, when we are at our best, it is because of our connection with God that we are able to do amazing things. It is because of our faith that we feed the hungry. It is because of our faith that we care for the planet. It is because of our faith that we work for justice in the world. And it is because of our faith that we come to church on Sunday, and we love one another.

Before any of this can happen, though, we need to be spiritually sup-ported. It is only when I am being fed spiritually, for instance, that my faith thrives. Likewise, when we are planted in good soil, nurtured by our faith, we are able to do good things in the world. And we make the soil good by connecting with God spiritually. That is what roots us, and what feeds us and gives us passion for the work we will do.

But when we let that soil grow dry, and when we stop growing spiritually and stop nurturing what grounds us and roots us, we find that we are like a vine that has stopped growing and that will no longer bear good fruit.

I have known churches like that. These are churches that are so busy that they forget why they are there in the first place. When they lose their connection with the spiritual they slowly lose the passion that once drove them. People don't tend to stay long in those churches because they get so burned out trying to work in dry soil.

Our churches and our denominations don't need to be like that. And neither do we. We do have good soil within us. But we are going to have to do some gardening first.

PLANTING SEEDS

How much attention does your church pay to the spiritual life? How often do you talk about how your soul is doing and what's going on spiritually for you? When you do, does it make you and your church uncomfortable? In fact, does it make you so uncomfortable that you wonder whether it might be easier to just do nothing at all?

Jesus used a lot of natural metaphors, including one about soil and seeds. In chapter 4 we talked about the man who threw seeds on the ground. Some fell on the path. Those were eaten by birds. Others fell on rocks. Because there was no depth to the soil, they quickly blossomed but then withered and died. Others fell in the thorns. When they tried to grow the thorns choked them to death. The last seeds, though, fell on good soil, and because of that soil they grew and yielded a great harvest.

Paul also talked about planting seeds. In his second letter to the Corinthians he writes with a piece of advice. "The one who sows sparingly will also reap sparingly, and the one who sows bountifully will also reap bountifully . . ." (2 Cor. 9:6).

But what both Jesus and Paul were saying is this: If you want to have a bountiful harvest, you have to plant. And if you want to plant, before you do anything you have to first have good soil. And even the best soil needs to be cultivated first.

Our spiritual lives are the soil onto which God's blessings are poured. The good news is that none of us is created with a bad soul, or bad soil. In fact, we are all created, as Genesis tells us, "very good," and we possess within ourselves ground in which God's Holy Spirit can move and create new life.

But it's easy to let our spiritual lives take a backseat. The fields of our hearts become overgrown with thorns. Our spiritual pastures become rocky ground. The soil that could once hold an abundance becomes eroded and shallow. Slowly the good soil is overwhelmed by the crush of life. Even in the midst of all of this, though, the good news is that we can always be transformed.

THE MISSING PIECE

After I just spent a chapter extolling the power of community, it may sound odd for me to now speak about the individual. The church community is at the heart of the Christian life, but the individuals who make up that community are not insignificant or interchangeable. In fact, the individuals themselves will define the community spiritually as either healthy or unhealthy.

Part of that health has to do with the spiritual transformations of the people in the church. In other words, is a given congregation a greenhouse for growing disciples? Or is it a place where growth has stopped? These are crucial questions because churches stagnate and die when they cease to cultivate disciples.

Evangelical churches often do discipleship well. When new members join the community they are literally taught how to be disciples. Bible studies are numerous. Prayer groups provide support for members. And newcomers are often "discipled" (meaning taught) by older members who act as mentors and companions on the faith journey.

Children and youth are taught to be disciples as well, and this formation often begins in the home. According to the National Study of Youth and Religion, "82 percent of children raised by parents who talked about faith at home, attached great importance to their beliefs, and were active in their congregations were religiously active as young adults." By contrast, "Just 1 percent of teens age 15 to 17 raised by parents who attached little importance to religion were highly religious in their mid to late twenties." One reporter who analyzed this study, David Briggs, concludes that parents "are far and away the biggest influence related to adolescents keeping the faith into their twenties."[8]

The question for progressive Christians is, how can parents do this work if they themselves are not equipped? This is often our problem. Because our churches lack Christian growth opportunities for adults, and especially for the increasing number of previously unchurched newcomers to the faith, parents have no idea what or how to teach their children.

Christian formation is instead relegated to a few hours on Sunday, if that, and then provided only by clergy and youth group leaders. Faith is not an everyday part of the family's language. By the time a young person raised in the church has reached adulthood, if the parents have been only moderately invested in the life of faith, the chances of remaining a highly committed Christian are virtually nonexistent.

At the same time, while our children and youth must always be a pressing priority for congregations, the spiritual life of the adult matters as well, regardless of whether or not children are a part of the equation. If a church becomes little more than a club, with no spiritual development taking place, there is simply no reason for the congregation to continue.

Community for no other reason than community is not a bad thing. It's great, in fact. But church members uninterested in the spiritual would be better served by a social club or other type of fellowship.

If, on the other hand, the people coming to our churches are looking for spiritual growth and meaning, the progressive church must step up its game. We may not agree with all of the beliefs of our more conservative siblings in the faith, but that does not mean we can't learn from them. We may understand discipleship to have a different end, but effective means are always worth examining.

THE FIRST AND SECOND PARTS

Progressive Christians, in so many ways, are very good at the second part of the Great Commandment: "You shall love the Lord your God with all your heart, and with all your soul, and with all your mind, *and you shall love your neighbor as yourself.*"

We really do try to love our neighbors well. I believe that at some level we are doing this because we understand that to love God we must also love our neighbors. At the same time, I sometimes wonder if we have so fully concentrated on the second part of that commandment that we have neglected the first.

Conservative evangelical churches, with their emphasis on one's "personal relationship with Jesus Christ," receive a lot of derision in progressive circles. Praise music in those traditions often describes a new Christian's developing faith in a way that makes it sound like they are falling in love with Jesus, in the most romantic of ways. Other times, Jesus is described as the best friend that we all wish we had.

There is a tendency to deride these relationships as shallow and self-centered. And I'll confess that "boyfriend Jesus" and "best friend Jesus" have never worked for me. But progressive Christians ridicule these relationships at our own peril. The truth is that while we might think that the conservative focus on building one's relationship with

God means we have the market cornered on love for our neighbor, we simply do not.

While many of us would not agree with some of the social platforms of more conservative Christians (antichoice, pro–"traditional family," etc.), it's a mistake to boil down the outreach of more conservative congregations to a handful of issues. The reality is that conservative denominations like the Southern Baptist Convention and Assemblies of God have hugely effective disaster response ministries. The Salvation Army has become practically synonymous with providing food and housing to those without homes. And the evangelically focused International Justice Mission has rescued literally thousands of women and children from sex trafficking.

Our conservative siblings do love their neighbors, and they often do so in ways that are far more effective than the efforts of progressive denominations. While we cannot ignore the fact that progressive denominations were responsible for some incredible social justice stands, such as an early religious response to the AIDS crisis and the welcome of LGBTQ individuals, there is so much more work to do.

Meanwhile, evangelical churches and denominations are even beginning to advocate for traditionally "liberal" causes. Opposition to the death penalty from evangelical Christians has increased, as have efforts to address the global climate crisis from a faith perspective. Meanwhile, while more traditional mainline congregations struggle with building and sustaining multicultural churches, evangelical denominations are welcoming growing immigrant communities and equipping members of those communities to serve as pastors.

Conservative evangelicals love their neighbors too. We may not always agree with how they do it, but we cannot say that theirs is a faith that concerns itself only with the first part of the great commandment. Instead we need to understand that why they do this, and how they sustain this work, has everything to do with the first part of the commandment. The key difference in so much of the social outreach done in more evangelical churches is that it comes deeply rooted in the love of God, the kind of love that deeply transforms and sustains ones belief in Christ into the work of loving one's neighbor.

So how do we progressive Christians do the same thing, but in our own way?

RECLAIMING SPIRITUAL PRACTICES

Cultivating our spiritual soil is all about cultivating our relationship with God. We all connect to God is different and worthy ways. But some methods have proven meaningful to Christians across the ages and are worth reclaiming as central to both our individual and corporate spiritual lives.

The corporate worship of God in community remains at the center of Christian life. Worship glorifies God by first praising God, and then equipping the people of God for the work of following Christ into the world and serving the world. At its best, worship can be engaging without simply seeking to be entertaining, deep without sliding into the esoteric and overly academic, and inclusive of people wherever they are on their spiritual journeys without being reductive to the point of meaninglessness.

There is no "right" worship style. Progressive Christians find meaning in everything from high Episcopal liturgies, to praise and worship services, to the hymns and sermons of traditional Reformed worship. Whichever format worship takes, though, in order for spiritual growth to occur there must be some sort of transcendent element that makes the time spent in worship different from simply another lecture, TED talk, or concert.

Preaching, in particular, can set the tone for the worship service. If sermons leave listeners feeling bored or baffled as to how it applies to their lives, the preacher has missed a golden opportunity. On the other hand, sermons that manage to inspire listeners to look for God's involvement in their everyday worlds can be life changing. If the hearers of a particular sermon can remember midweek what was said on Sunday and apply it to their day, that is evidence of powerful preaching.

But while the sermon is an important part of worship, especially in the Reformed traditions, it is not the only part. Corporate confession of sin, the sharing of prayers and thanksgivings, participation in the sacraments, and praising God in song all contribute to robust worship.

At its best, worship should gather the people of God together, help them to examine their lives, teach them through the proclamation and explanation of Scripture, join them together in prayer, and send them out into the world uplifted and ready to lift up the world. Worship that does these things will lay the groundwork for both an individual's and a congregation's spiritual life.

But our spiritual practices must not be confined to just corporate worship. Progressive Christians must also reclaim the spiritual practices that have too often been forgotten, such as the reading of Scripture, daily prayer, and Christian fellowship. The soil of the Christian life cannot be cultivated in only one hour a week.

We must reacquaint ourselves with the Scriptures, learning to read them in life-giving ways. Truly, many of us have been deeply hurt by those who have used the Bible to tear us down. It is tempting to respond by walking away entirely from what hurts us. But if we do that, we are ceding to the fundamentalist and literalist Christians of this world our birthright and inheritance.

Instead, progressive Christianity must help seekers to fall in love with Scripture. We must teach ways in which Scripture can both be read with twenty-first-century eyes and yet also be cherished as timeless. Scripture was never intended to be a history textbook or a science treatise. And yet, the well-meaning progressive phrase "I take Scripture too seriously to take it literally" has only succeeded in making sure no one takes it literally while failing to teach anyone how to take it seriously.

We have to stop being afraid of the Bible. Instead we should teach Scripture in a manner that reflects the whole of the Christian life by wrestling with it, seeking meaning, looking at things in new ways, and drawing strength from the journeys of our ancestors. Look for ways to integrate Bible studies into your church life. Encourage members to engage in daily Scripture reading. Do anything that will make the Bible less an object of fear, and more a companion and blessing on the journey.

Likewise, we must learn once again how to pray both individually and with one another. As a parish pastor I find that one of the things people are most afraid of doing is praying out loud. That makes some sense. Prayer is a deeply intimate act. Yet learning to pray with others can only help us to pray as individuals.

Especially when someone is new to the faith, hearing prayers out loud can be deeply helpful. When I was a young adult who had only recently come to the faith, progressive Christian mentors of mine would pray for me during my time of discernment. At first it felt a little odd to be prayed for like that. As time went on, though, those prayers became templates for my own conversations with God. I learned by example what it was to bring my whole self to my relationship with God and how to be able to drop any pretense of holiness or perfection in order to just be real.

We can model prayer for one another in community. We can also sustain one another through deliberate and regular prayer for each other. Small groups gathered around prayer have long been bastions of evangelical churches, for instance. Roman Catholic parishes have groups that gather regularly to pray around particular concerns. What would it look like in our progressive circles to have regular prayer partners or groups gathered around LGBTQ concerns, or environmental awareness, or peace?

Perhaps even more importantly, what would it look like to encourage prayer in our homes? Whether we live alone or with a family, there are always ways we can integrate prayer into our daily lives. Around the meal table, on daily walks, when we wake up or go to sleep, or when we are faced with a difficult decision, turning to prayer can become a routine that brings God closer in our day-to-day lives.

It is the responsibility of each person of faith to cultivate their own spiritual life. But it is the responsibility of the community of faith to give them the tools to do it. When a church or denomination fails to pay attention to the spiritual growth of individuals it's a lot like telling them to go prepare a field for planting while holding back the plough.

It's for this reason that I often disagree with clergy colleagues of mine who are upset when members leave their churches. They recount how those members told their pastors that they were "not being spiritually fed." In the pastor's eyes this often looks like a kind of selfishness, or a belief that church should be all about what a person gets out of it.

It's certainly true that sometimes members do leave churches for the wrong reasons. There is a big difference, however, between leaving a church because you are not being entertained versus leaving a church because you are not getting what you need spiritually. The first is selfish. The second is an indication of a real problem.

If a member of a church tells leadership that they are not spiritually growing under the church's care, it should be taken seriously, and serious changes should be made. This goes not just for congregations, but for entire denominations. Before we can do anything else, churches and denominations must be in the business of actively helping to create disciples. Disciples, people who are actively being transformed by the grace of God, are the body of the church. If we cannot build and sustain disciples, we cannot help to build and sustain anything else.

REAPING THE HARVEST

Earlier I wrote about Paul and his teaching that "you reap what you sow." I'll confess that I wrestle with that phrase. It has always sounded a little negative to me, like a threat or a warning that we might hear as kids from stern adults: "You reap what you sow, so if you don't study you're going to fail." Or "You reap what you sow, so if you don't floss you'll get cavities."

All of those things are true, but they aren't exactly inspiring. It's more like "Do this or else this bad thing will happen." In terms of motivating us to want to do something it ranks right up there with its close cousin "You made your bed and now you have to lie in it."

When you apply that message to the spiritual life, it sounds a lot like some stewardship sermons I've heard in the past. Those are the sermons where the message could be summarized by this: "You reap what you sow, so if you don't give to this church, we will not meet our bottom line and someday we will have to close our doors."

I've heard that sermon before. Verbatim. And I'm here to tell you that it has never inspired people to give more, or to grow spiritually. To tell you the truth, I think it does the opposite. If I ever happened to be a church member sitting out there in the pews and people told me that the only way to save my church was to open my checkbook so we could meet a bottom line on some spreadsheet, I wouldn't feel particularly inspired to give to that church.

To be perfectly honest, I hope you wouldn't be either. Here's why: A church that is just trying to meet a bottom line on a budget spreadsheet does not deserve your money. A church that exists only to fulfill its own needs and that worries only about maintaining the status quo and its own survival? That church doesn't deserve anything.

In fact, I'll go a step further. I would say that giving to a church like that is not only not helpful, but it's actually bad stewardship. Because of all the places doing good work that you could give to out there, giving to one that's focused only on self-preservation runs counter to building up God's realm and doing Christ's work in the world. Seriously, do not feel compelled to give to a church that cares only for its own survival, because that is not a church. That's just a clubhouse that is making the rest of us churches look bad.

I share this with you because stewardship is a good perspective for looking at the spiritual life. Too often in the church we think about stewardship only in terms of financial giving. But at its heart stewardship is really about all that we have, and how we choose to use it. That's because Paul is right; we really do reap what we sow. But don't hear that as a threat. Hear it as a challenge, and as hope.

Paul was writing this letter about planting seeds to a church. He wasn't really talking about literal seeds and harvests, of course. Paul was writing to ask the people of this church to support a new ministry in Jerusalem, and he knew that he was asking them to step out in faith and to imagine something that they couldn't see yet. He wasn't saying, "Hey, look, we are already doing this and we need some help meeting the budget." He was saying, "I believe God is calling us to do something new, and I'm asking you to give not because you have to, but because you believe in it."

In other words, this letter is Paul's stewardship sermon. He is telling the people that something great is possible, but he needs them to help him plant the seeds. The harvest, the tangible results that will come in a later season, will depend solely on this—what they are willing to plant now.

You reap what you sow. If you plant a few seeds, you might end up with something to harvest down the line. But what if you plant an abundance of seeds of hope in the soil of a place that is seeking to serve God in new and bold ways? That's how you end up with a bountiful harvest; but you can't get to that harvest by holding back.

And so that's the question we each have to ask ourselves as people of faith: What sort of harvest would I like to see, both in myself and in my church? And what am I willing to plant in order to get there?

What we choose to plant is what we will reap. What we decide to invest in our own spiritual lives will determine our harvest. So what we refuse to hold back, what we are willing to dare to let God transform, will yield a spiritual harvest that will sustain us for the transformation of our world.

That's not easy. And it shouldn't be. Because investing in our hopes is never an easy leap of faith, and when we decide to take that step and plant those seeds, we are indeed stepping out in faith. But when we plant seeds in this good soil, and we sow in faith, we will find that we can joyfully harvest an abundance.

We reap what we sow. That's true, and that is good news, because we can plant something amazing together.

7

GETTING OUR PRIORITIES STRAIGHT

GOTTA SERVE SOMEBODY

When I was in elementary school I read a lot of Choose Your Own Adventure books. The idea was simple. You started reading and after a few pages there would be a question for you to answer about how you wanted to proceed. You were given two different options, leading you to two entirely different pages in the book.

For instance, you are hiking in the woods and you are lost and it's getting dark. Do you keep trying to hike your way through? If so, turn to page 30. Or do you stop at the creepy abandoned cabin and stay there for the night? Turn to page 56.

As you can imagine, neither is a particularly good choice. But each choice leads you to other pages where you then have to make similar choices. Choice after choice, you work your way through the book and, to be honest, a good portion of the time you end up dying some tragic death.

Somehow someone thought these were great books for children.

Honestly, though, I was a big fan, and so were my friends. I think that's because the books always gave us choices, and they always took those choices seriously. Maybe that's why today I think about those books whenever I read the story that Jesus told about a father, his two sons, and the vineyard he owned (Matt. 21:28–31).

One day a father asked his sons to go to work in his vineyard. The first son said, "No, . . . I'm not going." But the second son said, "Sure, I'll go." Only here's the twist: The second son never goes, but the first son, who said he wouldn't, changes his mind and ends up going to work.

Jesus asks the Pharisees, "Which of those two sons did what his father asked? The one who said he would and didn't, or the one who said he wouldn't and did?"

The Pharisees answer, "The one who went to the vineyard."

And then Jesus delivers this stinger: "Truly, the tax collectors and prostitutes are going to be ahead of you in the kingdom of God." That's when the Pharisees get it . . . he's talking about them.

It's a dangerous thing to call out someone's hypocrisy. I don't suggest it because usually it makes the hypocrite pretty mad. But being Jesus has its privileges. He publicly exposes these religious officials, people who like the second son are a little more talk than action, for what they are, and it infuriates them.

There's something satisfying about that. There's a reason that when a person who professes religious faith falls from grace it becomes a media field day. As a young child I remember my parents watching televangelists be led off in handcuffs on the evening news. A few years later I looked around at some our more outwardly devout neighbors who weren't living in such devout ways when they thought no one was looking. I began to get a little disillusioned with religious people, and it struck me then that maybe not everyone's words and actions lined up.

Years later I've developed a little more sympathy for the Pharisees and other hypocrites of the world. That's because I know now that I'm a hypocrite sometimes too. More than likely, so are most of us. Perhaps my everyday hypocrisies aren't as newsworthy or spectacular as the ones on the front pages of the paper, but they are there. More than I like to admit.

The truth is that I call myself a Christian, or a follower of Christ. I say everyday that I will go to work in the vineyard, and most days I at least make it there. But some, I don't.

What does working in the vineyard look like? I think it looks like choosing to follow Christ, even when we are afraid, and even when there are other things we would rather be doing. And most importantly, even when it's hard.

I say I want to do that, but some days I know my own fears and limitations hold me back. I get distracted. I put my trust and faith in other things. I get it wrong. I know that some days I am so busy serving other gods and checking things off a to-do list, I never make it out to where I'm supposed to be.

My guess is that most of us who want to follow Christ have this problem. We have the best of intentions when we are called into the work our faith requires, but good intentions don't always get us there. Slowly we begin to realize that maybe, just maybe, we are hypocrites too.

This is where I am reminded of those Choose Your Own Adventure books—not because I think we are all headed for certain destruction (if so, this would be a pretty depressing book) but because I think that each day we get to make a new choice.

One of my parishioners quoted a song by Bob Dylan to me recently. In it he gives this long list of things that you might be—an ambassador, a rock-and-roller, a banker, or even a "preacher with your spiritual pride"—but he says no matter who you are "you're gonna have to serve somebody."[9]

It may just be a song, but he's right. We all end up getting to choose what, and who, we are going to serve each day. Each of us is asked the same question every morning when we wake up that was asked of the two sons: Will you go to work for me today?

It doesn't matter where our day takes us, or our profession, our age, or what we have or don't have in our bank accounts. It doesn't even really matter what you say when you are asked. All that matters is this: When you decide which vineyard to go to that day (and there are a lot to choose from), will you choose to work in one that belongs to something or someone who will never be able to love you back?

Or will you choose the vineyard that belongs to the one who loved you first, and always?

CHOOSING OUR OWN ADVENTURE

We often tell the children and youth of my congregation something I hope they will always remember: Never give the best of yourself to anything that can never love you back. I'm saying the same thing here too because I believe we are at a turning point for the progressive church. And like I've said before, it's time to make a choice.

We are coming to the bottom of a page where there are two options. One will take you to a page where things will carry on the way they always have. And the other will take you someplace that sounds scary, but may just be full of promise.

The thing about finding purpose, as individuals, as congregations, and as denominations, is that it is going to shift our priorities. Think about the major turning points in your life when your purpose shifted in a real way—marriage, having kids, committing to a career. Your priorities, how you spent your time and invested your energy, likely shifted as well.

Our churches, denominations, and movements all have priorities too, though we are often pretty foggy on what they might be. Too often we find ourselves adrift on seas of uncertainty and indecision and without the sail of purpose. Our priority becomes just staying afloat and not taking on too much water.

We can always raise that sail, though. If the progressive church is going to get serious about our purpose, the next step is going to be to take a hard look at our priorities. We are going to have to examine them in a meaningful and deliberate way. We are also going to have to make new choices, and go to pages of the book where we have never dared to turn before. Sometimes we're even going to have to throw out the old books altogether and write new ones.

Church growth experts are often fond of telling churches that they must have a mission statement or a vision statement or some other quick and pithy explanation of who they are and what they do. And I'm not saying that's a bad thing at all. It's better to know where you are aiming than to spin in circles. But these statements don't work if they are just glorified advertising phrases. They only work if we first get our priorities straight, and then commit to upholding them.

This is both an individual and a corporate practice. Personally, the idea that I am called to glorify God and live in joy because of God's love is what gives me purpose. That purpose is what helps me to set my priorities and live into them. Because I know my purpose, I'm able to thoughtfully decide what my priorities will be, and to then give my time and energy to them accordingly.

My purpose helps me to clarify my priorities and to make time for my relationship with God, my life with my family and friends, my work as a pastor and writer, and my continual renewal through sabbath rest. In a real way, knowing my purpose, setting priorities, and then attempting to live into them helps me to practice better stewardship of all I have been given.

Your purpose in life does not need to be identical with mine. But my guess is that it's probably not all that different. Your priorities are also bound to look a little different than mine as well, especially when it comes down to the details. But again, my sense is that if we are both trying to follow God's will for us, we are probably living diverse lives that nevertheless still share some common ground.

This exercise gets trickier, though, when we take it to the congregational level. All of a sudden hundreds of different possible understandings of a group's priorities and purposes are colliding. Many will match up, but there will be an inevitable back and forth taking place. It is in this jostling that congregations will have to make hard choices about which priorities will be put on the top of the list. This is why a clash of priorities is where most congregational conflicts begin.

This gets even trickier when we take it to the denominational level. Who dictates the agenda for an entire body of congregations? How are priorities set in a time when national funding is decreasing and mainline denominations face an uncertain future?

What results, in both congregations and in denominations and other wider church settings, should be a process of prayerful discernment. What often results instead is a power struggle between different groups with competing priorities who wage wars for control. While some healthy disagreement can be good for an organization because it helps us to truly determine our priorities, church conflict is sadly rarely like that.

Finding our priorities as individuals is a big part of what it means to be a Christian. But when we are called into community, which as Christians we always are, we need to continue that discernment in our congregations and denominations. This is why as Christian communities we need to learn how to have conversations about our priorities, and what we are willing to invest in our pursuit of them.

The problem is that we cannot do this work of setting priorities without first establishing a sense of purpose. I believe our lack of firm purpose has been a major part of the mainline decline of the last half century. We have been so murky about our purpose, so unsure about claiming our unique faith calling, that we have no common ground when it comes to priorities.

If the progressive church fails to positively define itself as a community of disciples, of Christ-seekers and Christ-followers, then we will never have the solid foundation of purpose that anyone hoping to set priorities needs. It will be like coming to the bottom of a page in one of those choose your own adventure books and finding that there are no choices. You'll just keep reading the same page over and over again.

On the other hand, if you and your faith community invest first in the work of becoming disciples, something amazing will happen. Your priorities will naturally and organically emerge. Differences in opinion will still exist, but communal discernment will come much more easily because you will be united in purpose. And if that purpose is rooted in Christ, you will find not only that your priorities are straight, but that you will have enough to live into them. And that move, from scarcity to abundance, will be life changing.

ENOUGH

When I was a college and seminary student in Atlanta there were two churches, both from the same mainline denomination, located on opposite ends of town. One church was very small. It only had about forty active members, and it was located in a neighborhood that for years had been considered down and out. For the life of them, no one could tell how that church managed to stay open year after year.

The other congregation was a very large church. In fact, it was the largest church in the entire denomination nationally. Each Sunday, in one of the most affluent neighborhoods in Atlanta, thousands of people streamed through its doors to worship.

You might think from this setup that I'm about to talk about David and Goliath, or the little-engine-that-could versus the huge monster no one could stop. But this isn't a story about good guys and bad guys, and it isn't about one defeating the other. This is a story about what it means to have "enough."

I'll come back to those two churches, but first there's another story to remember. In this one, Jesus and the disciples are being followed by a large crowd that wants him to heal them. As it gets later in the day, the disciples look out at the crowd and they start getting nervous. They see all these people and know they are about to get really hungry.

So the disciples say to Jesus, "Send them away . . . have them go and feed themselves." I'll bet that deep down the disciples were not just worried for the crowd. In fact, because Jesus was talking about giving everyone else something to eat, they were probably more worried that they wouldn't be able to hold on to the little they had for themselves. All they had with them were five loaves and two fish, which, when you think about it, was probably just enough for the disciples and Jesus to each have at least a little something. But Jesus was trying to give even that away!

So about now, if you put this in corporate terms, people could be saying that Jesus didn't have a very good business plan. He clearly did not have adequate supplies, and he hadn't budgeted well. Here he was at the height of demand, and he couldn't even meet the basic needs of the people who worked for him, let alone the consumers.

In short, Jesus simply did not have "enough."

The thing is, in Christ we find that our own definitions of "enough" rarely hold up. Jesus tells the disciples to bring the bread and fish anyway. He tells the thousands of people to sit down, and then he blesses the food and gives it to the disciples, who give it to the people. And, somehow, everyone on that hillside eats. In fact, they eat until they can't eat anymore, and then the disciples end up collecting baskets of the bread that hasn't even been touched.

It turns out that Jesus didn't just have enough. He had more than enough.

But how often does that happen? Here's a question to answer for yourself: Do you have enough? Could you use "just a little more"? Have you ever said to yourself, "If only I made a little more" or "If only I had this" or "If only I didn't need to deal with that" then you would finally have "enough"?

If so, you're not alone. Few people I have ever met, including people with extraordinary wealth, have ever thought they had "enough." In fact, sometimes those of us who have never had to think about having access to what others might find extraordinary, things like clean water and enough to eat and a home free of violence, are the ones who seem least aware of how close we really are to having "enough."

When times are the tightest, even in the church, we then want to hang on to what we have even more tightly. We become a little less generous with what little extra we have around, and we squirrel away what we don't really need. We hunker down and make sure that, at the very least, we will be okay. Then we stop taking even small risks, and slowly we stop focusing on the needs of our neighbors and start to look only at ourselves.

I think that Jesus knew what that was like, and so did his followers. As the disciples watched Jesus literally take their dinner out of their hands and give it away, I'll bet they were pretty anxious.

But Scripture says that when Jesus saw the crowds following him, crying out for healing, he had compassion for them. He doesn't say, "I don't have enough to give right now," and he doesn't send them away. Instead he finds what he does have to give, and he uses it to serve them.

Those two churches I told you about at the beginning of my sermon both did amazing things in their ministries. They both touched many lives. But that little church, the one with forty members, did something nearly unbelievable. Every night they invited homeless men in from the streets, and they let them sleep in cots in their sanctuary. They fed them hot meals, helped them secure housing and healthcare, and walked with them on their journeys.

The pastor of the larger church occasionally used to invite the pastor of the smaller one to speak in worship. The big church pastor was a good Christian who inspired his congregation to do great things, but he always struggled with the fact that his church never seemed to think they had "enough" to do more. Despite thousands of members and millions of dollars, there was always this sense of scarcity, and not abundance.

So when the small church pastor would come to tell the congregation about his ministry, the big church pastor would then slip in a mind-blowing fact, hoping his congregation might hear it. "You know," he would say, "this little church manages to do all this ministry every year on a church budget that is less than our own church's electric bill."

It was a sobering statement, and it brought into sharp contrast the difference between living a life ruled by the fear of scarcity and one driven by belief in God's abundance.

Just about every anxiety we have both as individuals and communities comes from the fear of not having, or being, "enough." Not rich enough. Not smart enough. Not good enough. Not creative enough. Not old enough. Not young enough. You get the picture.

Conversely, just about every extraordinary thing that is ever accomplished comes from trusting that we can make whatever we have be "enough." It's not recklessness or foolishness that gets us to that place. It's faith. That little church stepped out in faith and started their ministry, even though everyone called them foolish or crazy. Somehow the little that they had was blessed, and the world was blessed for it. Somehow, against all odds, there always seemed to be "enough."

We may not be sitting with that crowd on that hill, waiting for some bread and fish, but my guess is that we are all wrestling with what it means to have "enough," at least in some part of our life or faith.

The good news is that, like that crowd, we will find that when Christ is around we somehow always seem to have enough . . . in fact, if we look closely, we might just find that we have an abundance. Just like the overflowing baskets that were filled even after everyone was full, we will find that Christ somehow has blessed what we refused to hold back, and because of that we will find that we don't have to hold on out of fear anymore.

So here's my question for you today: What would you do if you finally believed that you had "enough"? Whatever that "enough" means to you, whatever it is "enough" of, what would you do if you felt like you had it? What would it mean to have "enough" as a church? And how might that "enough" bless the world?

LIVING IN BALANCE

I ask you that here because this chapter is the point in the book when we are getting serious about who we are. We are recommitting to a life of transformation because we are becoming disciples. We are finding our purpose, we are clarifying our priorities, and we are learning to live in faith and not fear.

It's that last part, living in faith but not fear, and living in a way that trusts that we have "enough," that is so often our biggest challenge. As people of faith we are called to be people of abundance, and not of scarcity. This does not mean that we will have more than others. This just means that we seek to use what we have in purposeful ways, and ways in which we will always seem to have been given more than enough.

Those questions about purpose and priorities and having enough resonate powerfully in today's culture. Finding "balance" is a topic that sells magazines and gets hits on blogs. Meanwhile, popular books tell us conversely to "lean in" while also telling us not to find our identity in our work. Parents are told that they are too involved, but then admonished for being too disconnected from their kids. And the phrase "work-life balance," and a promise to help someone achieve it, will sell just about anything.

Our larger culture is hungry for balance. Our church culture is as well. And, at its heart, any conversation on balance comes down to two things—setting the right priorities and believing you have enough.

Earlier I mentioned that we tell the children and youth at my church to never give the best of themselves to something or someone that will not love them back. That advice is good for every age. And, at its heart, it comes down to this: Never serve false idols. Instead, choose to serve God.

We all have false idols. Whether we admit it or not, we build our lives around the worship of things that can never love us back—addictions, money, work, bigger houses, more degrees on the wall, and more. The list goes on.

The hard truth, though, is that none of those things can ever love us back. They may give us happiness for a short amount of time, but it will always be fleeting.

When we reorient our life to put God at the center, we find that the other parts of our life begin to fall into line. Our relationships with others move back to places of importance. Our work becomes more meaningful. The way we use our money and other resources intuitively changes for the better.

So much of my preaching in my congregation focuses around living in abundance, finding balance, and setting priorities. I've been surprised to find that, more than any others, those sermons resonate. I think that is because we are all doing this work, and it is constant, lifelong work.

Learning to live in balance, and learning to live with the belief that we are and have enough, is a crucial part of what it means to live as disciples. We learn to love and be loved only by what can love us back. And in return, we find that we are better able to love the world.

In the past four chapters we have looked at what it means to be transformed by grace. We have talked about what it means to be a resurrected people, called into new life. And we have affirmed why being a part of a community of formation and learning matters.

But we have also discovered that disciples are people who seek to live with right purpose and priorities. Because of that, we also seek to live in balance and abundance, and in right relationship with God, one another, and our world. We are continuously growing and changing because of this, and so we will never stop being and becoming disciples, just as we will never stop being in relationship with God and others.

In the chapters that follow in part 3 we will begin looking at what it means for disciples to be active in the world. But before we could get to the next section, we first had to go through this section. We had to commit to being transformed people in order to become people of transformation. We had to let ourselves be changed and upheld by the grace of God. It is only because we have first done these things that we are now ready to take the next steps.

PART THREE

TRANSFORMING THE
WORLD WITH GOD

8

WEEKDAY CHRISTIANS

THE SECOND PART OF THE GREAT COMMANDMENT

One of my favorite places to go fly fishing is a stream in the Green Mountain National Forest in Vermont. As you follow the dirt road further into the woods, you pass cemeteries filled with those who are long dead and whose descendants have moved on. An old schoolhouse, unused for a hundred years, sits on the side of the road, restored but hardly visited. The once lively towns have been officially dissolved by the state. The bitterly cold and rocky terrain simply proved too difficult to live in, even for the heartiest of Vermonters.

But if you drive a little further, you find an orchard full of apple trees. Some farmer planted them in the 1800s, and they still bear fruit. Today they are allowed to remain because they provide ready food for the bears and other area wildlife to eat.

I am always amazed by that. Long after human beings gave up on the land and moved on, somehow those same acres manage to bear fruit every fall. The people who planted it, and their children, and grandchildren even, are all dead. But the soil is not. It feeds the trees, and each year a bounty comes once again.

That's the power of good soil. It is always capable of rejuvenation and growth. Because of good soil in our lives, what is planted in it can remain a source of blessing for others long after our life is over.

That's why we spent so much time in part 2 talking about why discipleship matters. If we root ourselves in soil that has been well cultivated, and if we sow the seeds of our life ambitiously, what we plant can be our legacy for generations to come. God can bless and multiply our works so that they become blessings for those we may never even meet.

Blessing others is what the second part of the greatest commandment is all about. As Jesus said, "You shall love the Lord your God with all your heart, and with all your soul, and with all your strength, and with all your mind; and your neighbor as yourself" (Matt. 22:37). Jesus even gave us the right order in which to do these things.

That's not because our neighbors are unimportant. On the contrary, it's because we are called to do the work of loving others that we first have to do the internal spiritual work, which connects us with God, and which makes us look at ourselves.

John Calvin, the father of the Reformed tradition, wrote in his *Institutes of the Christian Religion* that "true and sound wisdom consists of two parts: the knowledge of God and of ourselves."[10] As much as we have become a therapeutic culture (not a bad thing) some progressive church traditions have moved away from being inwardly reflective and have instead focused only on external action (also not a bad thing). In worship the moment of reflection during the corporate confession may be the only time in the service where we specifically are asked to look inward and examine ourselves. (And next time you're in church pay close attention to the turning of bulletin pages or other signs of nervous fidgeting during the silence.)

But in discipleship we turn to God first, and we turn inward so that later we may turn outward. If we are intentional about our own spiritual formation, we will see ourselves clearly, and we will also see that, even with all of our imperfections, we are beloved children of God. With that honest self-reflection, and the knowledge that God loves us and that the Holy Spirit is guiding us, we will become transformed people. That's incredibly important because transformed people can become people of transformation.

HAVING HAD A SPIRITUAL AWAKENING . . .

If you've ever been to an AA meeting, or another twelve-step group, you may have heard someone read from a piece of paper entitled "How it Works." Taken from AA's *Big Book*, this is a synopsis of the twelve steps recovering alcoholics are to take in the program. Step Twelve reads, "Having had a spiritual awakening as a result of these steps, we tried to carry this message to alcoholics and to practice these principles in all our affairs."

In other words, by the time recovering alcoholics get to the last of the twelve steps, what they have learned and how they have been changed is so extraordinary that they cannot keep it to themselves. Instead, they begin the work of sharing their recovery with others.

This is in contrast with the early steps when the newly recovering alcoholic first admits to having a problem, then turns to God (or their Higher Power, however defined), and then goes through the hard work of self-examination, truth-telling, and reconciliation. By the time they make it to the last three steps, which deal more with the maintenance of sobriety and service to others, it has become clear that one never really finishes working the twelve steps. It's a lifelong process, which each day is begun anew.

But what does any of this have to do with Christian discipleship?

In a real way the twelve steps of AA mirror the greatest commandment: love God, love yourself, and love your neighbor. Becoming a disciple is a form of healing; we are all broken by the world, but we get well by remembering that we are God's beloved creation, and by then reestablishing that connection. It's also a form of transformation; it is impossible to truly encounter God and to remain unchanged for the better. Because of both of these things, we become people who cannot help but to share our gratitude and joy with the world.

In chapter 2 we talked about the fact that Alcoholics Anonymous, a program with no advertising budget, has multiplied through the years simply because one member after another has chosen to "pass it on" to others. In the sobriety community it is understood that to receive recovery and not share that with those who still suffer is to be selfish. But, more than that, it is to sabotage your own recovery. It is because what AA calls "experience, strength, and hope" are shared with others that the person who shares them is able to constantly remember the grace that has been given to them.

It's the same with the love and grace we receive from God. When we truly experience it, we simply cannot keep it to ourselves. We must share it with the world through our lives and our actions. It is when we start doing this consistently that we know we have begun to live out the second part of the greatest commandment.

LIVES OF GRATITUDE

When I was in seminary, at a deeply Reformed theological school of the Presbyterian Church, it was drilled into us that grace and gratitude were intimately related. God's grace is abundant, and the only proper response that we have as people who have received that grace is gratitude. Because we have been touched by grace, we work to glorify God. Most importantly, we do all of this not because we have to, but because we sincerely want to do so.

In my own life I have received more than a little grace. God's grace has been, as the hymn says, amazing. That is not to say that it has eradicated difficult times or suffering, but it has transformed those rock bottom times into pathways for new life. More importantly, that grace has transformed me and reminded me that even in the darkest of times Christ's light still shines.

I understood grace and gratitude in the academic sense in seminary, but it wasn't until a few years later that I really got it. The first time I truly understood what "Amazing Grace" meant, I felt blown away. I'd sung the hymn many times, but I'd never really understood the words: "through many dangers, toils, and snares, I have already come. 'Tis grace has brought me safe thus far, and grace will lead me home." This time I felt the hymn's true meaning in every part of my being.

It was around the same time that I gradually came to understand what it means to live life in gratitude for God's grace and love. Some of my seminary professors called this "living your life as a thank you to God," and I think that's as apt a description as any. Life becomes not something in which we hope to glorify ourselves, but instead something in which we strive with every grateful action to glorify God.

Put another way, because we have been transformed by the grace of God, we become transformative people, seeking to gratefully change the world for the better.

In the worship services of many of the traditions that make up the progressive church, the liturgy itself bears this out. After we have gathered around the Word of God, have prepared to hear and then have heard the proclamation of the Word in Scripture and preaching, and have responded to the Word in prayer, giving, and sacraments, we are then asked to do one more thing: follow and bear the Word out into the world.

The Word of God is often understood as just Scripture, but the Word is much bigger than that. As John says, "In the beginning was the Word," and that Word is Christ, or God incarnate. So as people who are transformed by Christ, we are asked to both follow the Word and carry the Word out into the world.

This does not mean that we are bringing Jesus to people. Jesus Christ is already in the world; we just need to have eyes to see him. It does mean, though, that we are trying to follow Christ out into the world. It also means that we are bringing our own selves, which have been transformed by God's love and grace, into the world, and we are seeking to do good.

We do this not because we have to, but because we are so grateful to God that we cannot help but love our neighbors enough to want their lives to be good too. Gratitude thus becomes the place where our actions are rooted. It becomes our motivator and the source of our endurance.

Our gratitude enables us to do the things that not only make the world a more just and peaceful place, but that also bring glory to God. In a real way, gratitude is what connects the first and second parts of the greatest commandment. It roots our actions in God's love and grace, and it pushes us past our own self-interests into the transformation of the world.

LIVING OUR LIFE AS A PRAYER

But changing the world is a tall order. It's absolutely overwhelming, if we are being honest with ourselves. Where do we even start?

That's a question I often get as a pastor. "The world is so broken," someone will say, "What difference can I even start to make?" There's never a perfect answer. At best, we are left feeling helpless, and at worst we slip into nihilism. The whole task just feels too big.

That's why we can only do this: start where we are, with our own lives and in our own homes and communities. And we start by praying.

I understand that prayer might feel difficult, amorphous, and less than helpful in the face of concrete problems. I've certainly felt that way. In fact, when I was in college I was having a hard time praying. I'd try to sit still and concentrate on God but, to be perfectly honest, that never lasted for more than a minute or so. I'd start to pray, my mind would drift off, and before long I'd forget I was praying at all.

At this point it's okay if you think I was not a very spiritual person. Believe me, I did too. So I went to my college chaplain and asked why I couldn't seem to pray the way that others did. Was something wrong with me?

He surprised me with this challenge: "Instead of worrying about how you are praying, why don't you try living your life as a prayer?"

Prayer, he explained, is not just about bowing our heads and being alone with God (though there certainly is a place for that). Instead, prayer is about being connected with God in all of our lives, including in our actions.

Prayer is more than just holy words. That's one reason why I often get frustrated when I hear people saying someone or something is in their "thoughts and prayers" when something difficult happens. Thoughts and prayers are great, but they are not true prayers if the one saying them doesn't actually intend to do anything beyond saying a few words. Prayer is not just about thinking about something for a moment. It's not sending a quick message to God the way we might send an e-mail, getting it off of our desk and onto God's.

Instead, prayer is about joining ourselves with a cause and choosing to invest in it with our lives. It is not something that is over the moment we say "amen." "Amen" means "truly" after all, as in "I truly mean this God." And so, in a profound way, when we say "amen," that really means we are just getting started with the praying.

So many of the prayers we begin on our knees, in silence, or with bowed heads can continue after we say "amen." That's when we "truly" begin living them out as we draw on the strength and wisdom we have prayed for to do the work of transforming the world for good. Our prayerful actions deepen our spiritual connection with God profoundly and lead us to participate in the world in powerful ways.

Prayer at its best is not disconnected from the world. It is not meant to just be a personal affair. Indeed, prayer becomes lived faith—a kind of faith that can change the world.

BEYOND SUNDAYS

The problem is, if that's true, it's tempting to think that our actions must always be grand. We look at those who have risked their very lives in order to transform the world, like those who crossed the Pettus Bridge in Selma, Alabama, and think "that is prayer in action." When we then look at our own lives, we might feel a little deflated and irrelevant.

But it's in our day-to-day lives, and not just those most extraordinary days, where our true faith is revealed. So if we want to become people who live their lives as prayers, we have to start by first looking past Sundays and toward the holiness of each day.

I talk about this a lot during Holy Week. It's a long week with added church services that leave even those who gain renewed energy from worship tired. Clergy often take one of their vacation weeks the following week in order to recover. And we pastors, regardless of whether we admit it or not, know that when we announce the additional Holy Week services some people are groaning a little inside.

I get it. We're all busy. Sunday morning feels hard enough for many good Christians. Thursday night, after a long day at work, is even tougher. You just want to go home, have dinner, and either tackle the pile of laundry or have a few precious hours to yourself. You probably don't want to take the car out one more time, drive to church, and sit through another service.

I confess to sometimes feeling the same way, but the occupational hazard of being clergy means we can't just call off during Holy Week. That means the messages of the stories we hear on Maundy Thursday and Good Friday can't go unheard by us.

That's good because what we hear about Jesus on those two nights is the same as what we hear every day in our pastor's studies or our offices. We don't talk about that much, and that's too bad. Most churches are good at doing Sundays, but sometimes even those of us who are clergy are not so good at acknowledging what comes between Sundays.

On Sunday mornings we focus on the joy. We sing uplifting hymns. We hear hopeful sermons. We smile. We shake hands. We dress up. We talk about grace and blessings and gratitude. That's not a bad thing.

But when many loyal churchgoers leave on Sunday, they step into a different world. Between Sundays I visit with people who are facing a struggle that few in their lives know about, and even fewer understand. They're sick or injured, dying or bereaved, depressed or heartbroken, betrayed or alone, or just plain wrestling with doubt. The problem is that if you come to church only on Sundays, you might not think we in the church know anything about that.

Come between Sundays on Holy Week, though, and you'll find a faith that knows what those struggles and personal experiences are like. More than that, you'll find a God who knows what they are like. To me, the most comforting part of Holy Week is not the waving of triumphal palms on one Sunday morning, or the flowers and joyous hymns on the next. It's what happens in between.

Church is Jesus on Maundy Thursday sharing a table with the people he loved the most. It's him washing their feet and showing that the mark of a true leader is whether they can serve others. It's also Jesus still loving his disciples even though he knew that, at best, they would abandon him, and at worst, they would betray him. And it's Jesus in the garden, alone, heartbroken, and struggling between what he wanted to do and what he knew he had to do.

Church is also Jesus on Good Friday when he world turns against him, and the ones who cheered his entry in Jerusalem now cheer his death instead. He suffers. He calls out to a God who does not seem to answer. He doubts. He feels pain, and loss, and grief. And in the end he loses the life he knew.

I'm sometimes asked by those who are going through a difficult time whether God is angry when they have doubts, or when they wonder why God doesn't seem to be answering prayers. They ask if God understands when we suffer, or when we feel alone.

When they do, I point first not to the Christ of Palm Sunday or Easter, but to the weekday Christ. The one who lived as one of us, who loved as one of us, who doubted as one of us, who suffered as one of us, and who died as one of us. Only then do I point to the Christ who rose again and overcame the worst that the world could throw at him.

I sometimes worry that we are forgetting how to be Christians on weekdays. As more churches cancel even midweek Holy Week services due to low attendance and overscheduled members, and we instead roll all the stories into a Passion Sunday service on Palm Sunday, I wonder, are we losing that time we once had to sit with Christ in his own human struggles? I also wonder if when we lose that time we then also lose our ability to learn to sit with others in their struggles, and with ourselves in our own.

But what would Christian life look like if we took that time? What if we became known not just as the people who knew what to do on Sundays, but as the ones who knew how to stay with you when your life was falling apart, just as Christ asks us to do on Maundy Thursday? Or the ones who could stand by and still love and respect you even when you call out your doubts, just as Jesus did on the cross? What would happen if we weren't just known for our Sunday celebrations, but for our Thursday night solidarity, or our Friday afternoon compassion?

C. S. Lewis wrote in *Mere Christianity* that Christians should become "little Christs" to one another and to the world, affirming that "the whole purpose of becoming a Christian is simply nothing else."[11] We are called to love, advocate for, and serve others the same way that Christ does. In our everyday lives, from the grocery store to the office to the school pickup line, we are asked to be daily, embodied reminders of God's grace.

Rest assured, we will not do this perfectly. We are going to mess up every single day, and we are never going to get it exactly right. But we keep trying, because our faith compels us to do nothing less, and not just on Sundays, but on the days between. The world has plenty of Sunday morning Christians. It needs a few more of the weekday ones.

FRUIT OF THE APPLE TREE

This chapter started by talking about apple trees, and now we've come full circle. So here's a question for us as we end: What is the fruit of an apple tree?

If you're like most people (or at least like me) you'll give the obvious answer: an apple. But I was once listening to a talk by the Rev. Jack Stephenson, senior pastor of Anona United Methodist Church. He asked this same question and then said something that struck me: "The fruit of an apple tree is another apple tree."

Think about that for a minute. An apple contains seeds that, when planted in good soil, can grow more apple trees. The fruit is delicious, but its lifespan is short. It is the seeds that hold the real potential.

I told this story in a sermon once and one of my church's members, a man who had grown up on a farm, told me a story about his grandfather. They were walking around the farm together when they passed by some rotting apples.

"What do you see?" the grandfather asked.

"Rotten apples," said the son.

"No son," he replied, "that's another tree."

That lesson had stuck with him his whole life. It also resonates for the Christian life. It's a reminder to us all to never discount what God is capable of doing with potential, and to never underestimate the ways that God is able to multiply the tiniest of offerings into abundance.

As disciples who have been transformed, we are now called to be transformational people in a world that is so in need of more love, justice, mercy, and peace. In a real way, we are called to plant seeds that we may never see fully bloom in our lifetimes. More than that, we are planting for neighbors we haven't met yet, and in fact may never have the chance to know this side of the reign of God.

And yet, every day we cast those seeds out into the world. We do it with grateful hearts, touched deeply by grace. And we do it as people who are called to live our lives both as prayers and as thank-you notes to a God who loves us so much that we cannot help but to love our neighbors.

When our lives become more focused on gratefully planting trees for others rather than on keeping the fruits of the harvest for ourselves, that's when we know this discipleship thing has started to take hold. And that's also when we know that we will never settle for anything less than abundant life ever again.

9

STATEHOUSE HALLWAYS

In June of 2011 my future wife and I spent a week in the halls of the New York State Capitol building along with a crowd of other marriage equality supporters. Before state bans against same-sex marriage started tumbling, before the Defense of Marriage Act was overturned, and before the Supreme Court declared that marriage equality was the law of the land, there was the fight for equality in New York state. New York's anti-gay marriage laws were the lynchpin in the struggle, the big domino whose fall would signal that victory nationwide was in sight.

My wife is a native upstate New Yorker, which made this extra personal to her. So day after day we drove from our home, then in southern Vermont, to Albany, where we joined the chorus of witnesses asking for marriage equality to come to New York.

The first day, when I showed up in my clergy collar, the anti–equal marriage crowd saw me and smiled. They assumed I was one of them.

But when Heidi and I stood next to a group of radical queer activists wearing pink tape over their mouths to signify the silencing of same-sex couples, more than a few eyebrows were raised.

The halls of the building were filled to capacity with protestors on both sides. Each day for the next week we endured what can only be described as verbal abuse from anti-equality Christians. Truly, not all of those opposing marriage equality were mean spirited. Some were nice enough, and went so far as to offer us water and snacks. Too many others, though, were just plain unkind, and too few of the good Christians who stood nearby did anything to rein them in.

The most harrowing moment for me came when a prominent ex-gay activist pointed at my clergy collar and yelled, "You're not fooling anyone with that thing!" He yelled that I was not a real pastor, and that I had simply bought a clergy shirt to try to deceive others.

When I replied that I was an ordained minister he looked incredulous and told me to read the Bible. (I let him know that I'd read it cover to cover, in English and the original Hebrew and Greek.) Fuming, he told me I was going to hell. Before I could respond Heidi grabbed my shoulder and guided me away.

The incident left me shaken, not so much for me, but for Christians everywhere. Too often progressive Christians have ceded the public proclamation of Christian values to conservatives and fundamentalists. If you asked the youth and young adults who were with us in that hallway that week what Christians thought of them, they would likely have believed that the vast majority of Christians hated them. That was true, even with Heidi, myself, and a moderate number of other supportive clergy visible and engaged.

This is probably not all that surprising to you if you are a progressive Christian. If you're anything like me, you roll your eyes in frustration every time a right-wing extremist clergy person claims to offer the "Christian perspective" on an issue. Or, like me, you may wonder how the freedom to bully and abuse LGBTQ youth ever became a "religious liberty" issue dear to the hearts of Christ's followers.

The public hijacking of the name "Christian" by those who would use the government and other means to limit the rights of others is a threat not only to our democracy, but also to our faith. The simple fact is that too often the word "Christian" is understood in our culture to be synonymous with "unkind," "judgmental," or "exclusionary." The most distressing part is that though progressive Christians are a smaller group than more conservative and fundamentalist Christians, we have not ceded our place in the public arena sheerly because we are outnumbered.

It is my belief that a big part of the reason so few people know about progressive Christians and our churches is because we don't know who we are and for what we stand. Most of us would be hard-pressed to make an elevator speech about why we are a Christian and what that means for how we interact with the world. We prefer instead to say what we *are not.*

But the problem with defining ourselves mostly in negatives is that it leaves us little solid ground on which to stand. In an age of rootlessness when people are looking for meaning, that's just not enough. Not only will we not thrive, but progressive Christianity might not even survive.

Of course, we have another choice. Up until this point we have looked at ways to become disciples, people who are formed and transformed by our relationship with Christ, our teacher. Now we are continuing our turn to the next stage of faith development: becoming a witness to Christ, and using our witness to transform the world.

ROLLING AWAY THE STONE

But where do we start? For me, the answer to that question is "at the empty tomb."

I know good progressive Christians who hold completely divergent views of the Resurrection of Jesus Christ. Some believe that Jesus was literally resurrected from the grave. Others believe a sort of spiritual resurrection took place. And others believe that the resurrection that happened was the community that gathered around Christ's memory after his death. Still others admit that they think something happened, but they just don't know what or how.

I'm a believer in the literal Resurrection personally, but if you are not, that's okay. Resurrection can be a metaphor that guides you in your Christian journey nonetheless. That's because at its heart resurrection is about things every Christian should value: hope, grace, new life, and the triumph of love over the forces of oppression.

So, think about Easter Sunday at your church. It's the day of resurrection. Flowers and trumpets. Easter egg hunts and the Alleluia chorus. It is a day of joy, one without compare, and if your church is like mine, no celebration is too big on this holiest of Sundays.

But, just as in the last chapter, before we get to Sunday, we have to get through Thursday.

Each Maundy Thursday we have our annual Tenebrae service at the church I serve. In that service the gospel story of Christ's last hours is told in pieces, and one by one the lights in the sanctuary are lowered until we are left in almost total darkness. We then leave the sanctuary in silence and we wait for Good Friday, and for the day when the world did the worst it could to a man who was God's love personified.

We do that in the church during Holy Week. We go through the motions of remembering Christ's betrayal, and suffering, and death. We do this not just because we are remembering something from the past, something that happened all those centuries ago, but in a larger way because we are telling a story that still makes sense today.

As many other theologians have said before, though Christians are Easter people, we live in a Good Friday world so much of the time. We live in a world where violence, addiction, injustice, hatred, and poverty all too often surround us. This is a world where we see pain and suffering up close, and a place where some days we may feel just as dark as the tomb was all those centuries ago.

But . . . what if it doesn't have to be that way?

The Gospel passage we traditionally read on Easter tells us that on the morning after the Sabbath, on the first day that they could, three women went to the tomb where Jesus had been buried. One of them was Mary Magdalene, and another was Mary, the mother of Jesus. They went on Sunday because they hadn't been able to properly prepare Jesus' body for burial on Friday and so there they were, his mother and two women who had loved him, grieving deeply for him and for all the hope they had lost when he died.

That day they were trying desperately to just be able to say goodbye properly; to just have that one moment. And as they walked they had one big problem: They didn't know how to roll the stone away from the tomb. That was a problem because in front of the tomb, the people who had buried Jesus had put this huge, heavy boulder blocking the entrance, one the women had no idea how they were going to move.

It was while they were still trying to figure out how to do it, while they are really just talking about logistics, that they came upon the tomb and discovered something shocking: the stone was gone! As they walked into the tomb, Jesus was nowhere in sight. Instead a man dressed in a robe just sat there.

Scripture tells us that the women were "alarmed."

That's one way to put it. My guess is that as they stood there in that empty tomb, with a stone inexplicably rolled away and the body of their son and brother gone, they were more than a little "alarmed."

And the guy in the glowing white robe, the one they've never seen before, very helpfully says to them, "Don't be alarmed!" He goes on, "You are looking for Jesus of Nazareth, who was crucified. He has been raised. He is not here."

He tells the women to go on ahead to Galilee and tell the other disciples. And he tells them, "You will see him there!" But Scripture tells us that they did something that may seem surprising: they ran away, and they were afraid.

The three women had just seen the most unimaginable, amazing thing ever. They'd been given news that was literally unbelievable. And contrary to the way we think of Easter, their first reaction was not joy or awe or celebration. It was alarm. And fear.

Truth be told, I think I would be alarmed too. Because none of this makes sense. Stones don't roll away on their own. People don't rise from the dead. And—this is the big one—we don't get the kind of second chances that they'd just been given.

Because that's what resurrection is all about. It's about second chances. It's about a new lease on life. It's about the world meeting God's love in the flesh and responding not with joy but with fear. And it's about that love still having the last word anyway, and not to condemn us but to love us even more.

It's about the biggest, heaviest, most immobile stones in our lives being rolled aside like they are nothing. Because, compared to God's love for us, they are. Most Christians would say that the cross is the sign of our faith. But I've heard it said before that maybe there should be another one. Maybe it should be a stone, because in the end even the cross could not destroy God's love. It is the rolled-away stone that tells us that truth.

So two thousand years later, despite all that has happened since, despite every attempt of the world to roll that stone back and seal love into that tomb, it hasn't happened yet. Even in the hardest of days, God's love still somehow rises again.

ALARMED AND AMAZED

That is amazing. And, truth be told, it's alarming. Here's why: Because it means there is hope. And hope is messy business.

It's messy because hope does make you change your plans. Hope makes you go from someone who is walking to the tomb of a friend to perform one of the saddest final acts of love imaginable to someone who is running from the graveyard believing that maybe, just maybe, what that man in white said is true. Maybe the Resurrection is real.

You go from accepting as inevitable the worst-case scenario to believing in the possibility of new life. You also go from the comfort of complacency to the affliction of knowing there is something better waiting.

Resurrection is joyful.

Eventually.

But truth be told, first it shakes you up and it changes everything. It is "alarming." But maybe that's not such a bad thing.

I was curious about that word "alarmed," so I went back to the original language, the Greek in which the New Testament was first written. And like so many things, that word doesn't exactly translate well. The original word that was used when they first wrote this story down can mean "alarmed" but it can also mean something else—"amazed."

I don't think it's an accident that you can confuse the two. Because when it comes to resurrection, when it comes to the new life that is offered in Christ's love, "alarmed" and "amazed" are two sides of the same coin. It is amazing, but the alarming part is that once you know resurrection, nothing will ever be the same again.

The truth is that at some point in our lives we have all been in the tombs. We have given up hope, we have felt pain, and we have lost what we loved. Maybe we have questioned how a world can allow so much suffering. And, perhaps, we've wondered where God is in all of it.

That's human, and that's what any good person would ask. But it's also not the end of the story. The end of the story, and the start of a whole new one, comes from the man who sits in that same tomb saying, "He's not here . . . he's been raised."

So the blessing and the challenge is that you get to choose whether you will be too. You too are a part of this resurrection, because you too are called to be a resurrected person. You are called to something better with God. And it may at times be alarmingly difficult, but it will also be amazing.

It is amazing because resurrection is everywhere if you look for it, and it's waiting for you to walk past the rolled-away stones, come out into the world, and be a part of it too. We have all been invited to this resurrection, and when we truly understand that, then we will be so amazed that we won't be able keep silent. When that happens we will then have to become witnesses to all that we have seen.

WITNESSES TO THE RESURRECTION

The word "witness" probably sounds a bit like insider language, though. It's not a word many of us use regularly, unless we are thinking about the legal sense of the word, like a witness to a crime or a witness for the defense. Or, if you've heard it used in a church setting, it may have been tied to proselytizing others: "We are going to go witnessing to try to find converts."

That's not what I'm talking about here. Instead, being a witness to Jesus Christ has more to do with the idea of "attraction versus promotion" that we talked about earlier. It's about taking the light out from under the bushel basket and letting it shine in the world. Or, as the Book of Acts puts it, "We cannot keep from speaking about what we have seen and heard" (Acts 4:20).

In other words, when something has impacted us so deeply, changed us so radically, and turned our world inside out for the better, we can't help but to live out our faith in every part of our life, including the public part.

Let me first be clear about what this does not look like. This is not about pushing our beliefs or our way of life on others. This is not about Christian superiority. And this is not about street-corner evangelism.

This is, however, about how we bear witness to what God has done in us. It's about how we live our public lives, and why we make the choices we do. Being a witness is about changing the world, but it's also about how we have been changed. That's a little different than just being church people who are involved in social justice. This is about being people who have been fundamentally transformed by the good news of Jesus Christ and who now can do nothing except advocate for God's love, peace, and justice for all.

This is about being people who, in the words of Martin Luther, take their places at the forefront of every movement for good and proclaim, "Here I stand. I can do none other."

Karl Barth kept a painting above the desk where he wrote his voluminous *Church Dogmatics*. It was a copy of Matthias Grunewald's painting *The Crucifixion*. As the title indicates, it's a portrayal of the death of Christ. But the most interesting thing about this painting is what John the Baptist is doing in it. Standing to the side, he is holding a copy of the Scriptures and pointing to Jesus.

Barth is said to have seen great meaning in that. John, who had already drawn quite a following to himself, refused to let himself be the focus. Instead, he pointed only to Jesus in all that he did. He was one of the first witnesses to Christ.

Barth's books talk extensively about being a witness to Christ. Throughout his volumes of work it is a consistent theme. But his interest in the concept of being a witness was far more than academic. In fact, it spurred Barth on to work against one of the greatest social evils of modern history: National Socialism in Germany.

In 1934, as the Nazis continued to gain power and impose totalitarianism in Germany, Barth and others in the Confessing Church movement (those who opposed the Nazi takeover of the churches in Germany) gathered to draft and adopt a document stating their dissent. The statement they issued, called the Theological Declaration of Barmen, was a confession of Christian belief that explicitly rejected Adolf Hitler and his reign and instead declared Jesus Christ as Lord.

As the declaration reads, "Jesus Christ . . . is the one Word of God whom we have to hear, whom we have to trust and obey in life and death."[12] Not Hitler, not National Socialism, and not a totalitarian state. The document concludes with these words: The Word of God will last forever. The implication is clear: Hitler will not.

THE RISK OF BEING A WITNESS

It was a risky thing for any person to do. In many ways it was far riskier than anything North American Christians today who are committed to social justice will ever be asked to imagine. All of the Christians who took part in the crafting of the document knew that they were taking their own life into their hands.

And yet, in the face of such profound evil, they had no choice but to proclaim the great truth that they knew: Jesus Christ, the incarnate Word of God, was greater than Hitler. Their Christian faith required that followers of Jesus explicitly reject Naziism and vocally proclaim their loyalty only to Christ. The followers of Christ who would stand up against Hitler, including Barth, were willing to risk everything to witness to Christ.

To return to the example of the martyred Dietrich Bonhoeffer, contemporary Christians must remember that there is indeed a "cost of discipleship." The time to pay that cost often comes when a disciple moves from private reverence to a public witness of faith. It is in discipleship that we learn who we are, but it is in witnessing that we display our discipleship in concrete and visible ways.

For Bonhoeffer the cost of his discipleship was his own life. That is still a price that some Christians pay in parts of our world. But for most of us in North American settings, expressing our faith is not a threat to our existence.

And yet, Bonhoeffer was right when he said, "When Christ calls a man, he bids him come and die."

Most of us will not be asked to pay that price with our actual lives. But Christians, and American Christians in particular, must learn how to once again be willing to be uncomfortable for our faith.

That's a hard sell in a culture where even perceived slights will make some Christians jump up and yell "persecution!" Except, really, we modern American Christians are pretty darn comfortable. And don't tell your angry uncle who is railing against gay marriage and political correctness at Easter dinner this, but calling yourself Christian in our culture is one of the easiest things you can do.

That's too bad, because the church actually doesn't do very well when things are easy for it. Look back at nearly every time the church has been on the wrong side of history: the Crusades, the Spanish Inquisition, slavery, the suppression of gay rights. What do all of those things have in common? When each happened, the church was in a position of having great strength and influence in society.

But on the other hand, look at the times churches got it right: Black Christians in the civil rights movement. Dietrich Bonhoeffer and the Confessing Church in Nazi Germany. Oscar Romero standing at the altar. They were hated, targeted, outnumbered, and sometimes they may as well have signed their own death warrants. Yet they were being the church in a way few of us ever will.

The church does not thrive in comfort. The church thrives when it is being called to the messy and painful work of transforming the world. Why? Because that's when we are witnessing to the One who transcends all the injustice of the world, and who gives us strength to teach a new way.

The trouble is that too many of us believe that faith should be something that requires nothing of us. So if discipleship is a hard sell, then witnessing to Christ in ways that make us uncomfortable is going to be even harder.

But Christ never called us to comfort, and Christ's call should never be misinterpreted as one that allows us to be unchanged. Instead, Christ calls us to something better than comfort. He calls us to our true selves.

The word the original Greek New Testament most associates with "witness," or having a "testimony" of Christ, is *marturia*. It's the same word that we've come to understand as "martyr." That is what the martyrs of the faith over the centuries, people like Dietrich Bonhoeffer, are at their core: they are witnesses to the faith who, even in death, still testify to Christ's love, justice, and grace.

I'm not saying that you and I need to die for our faith. Not exactly, anyway. But I am saying that in discipleship we have to allow some of our assumptions and beliefs to die. We have to reexamine our lives, and how we always believed they would look, and then ask whether they are truly glorifying God. Then finally we have to look at the world around us, one in which we ourselves may be quite comfortable, and be willing to choose to be less comfortable on behalf of others.

RESURRECTION PEOPLE

When we choose to do this work, the work of witnessing not for ourselves but for others, then we become witnesses to Christ's love and justice on behalf of the world and for the world. This is not about making the world better for ourselves, though surprisingly often that will happen as well. This is about reenacting Christ's love for all in our actions.

Each of us can likely find a place in our own lives where our faith is pushing us out of our comfort zones. In my life I have recently been asking how I can do this in the midst of the Black Lives Matter movement. I am white, which in the country where I live gives me a tremendous amount of unearned privilege. I have never been told that "white lives matter" or "all lives matter." That's because no one ever had to tell me those things. They were communicated to me from the moment I was born in a myriad of ways.

But now I am hearing my African American friends and neighbors telling their truths in new ways, and with a new urgency. I am listening. And I am trying to become a good ally in the struggle.

I do this because, as an openly gay person who is now able to marry the woman I love, I know that none of that would be possible had others not worked for my rights. I'm particularly grateful for those Christians who spoke out not in spite of their faith, but because of it. They were witnesses to Christ's love for all, and they made this world better.

Now I am trying to be a witness for Christ's love and justice too, only this time in the pursuit of civil rights and racial justice. I am also relearning the lesson any would-be ally needs to learn: you are not an ally if you are not willing to risk something for the cause. In other words, if being an ally costs you nothing, you are not an ally.

Conveniently this is the same thing that discipleship asks of us. If it costs us nothing, if we are not willing to bear it out through acts of public witness, then we are not disciples. We do this not to save others, but to proclaim the saving grace, love, and justice of a God who is still at work in the world.

Why? Because, as so many others have said, we are indeed Easter people. We are people of the Resurrection. And because we are disciples, people transformed and taught by Christ's love, then we are resurrected people as well. In discipleship we have died and continue to die to the things that would destroy us, and we instead find our true selves again and again in those things that will give us truly abundant life.

We who would be Jesus' disciples must also be something more. We must be witnesses in a world that is very desperately in need of the kind of love, justice, and mercy that Christ embodies. We must be people willing to be made uncomfortable for the gospel, and for others. We do this work of witness not because it is a nice or good thing to do, though it is those things too. We do it because we are disciples, and as Luther would say, "here we stand. We can do none other."

IO

PENTECOST PEOPLE

WHY ARE WE HERE?

"Love is patient, love is kind . . . It bears all things, believes all things, hopes all things, endures all things . . . And now faith, hope, and love abide, these three; and the greatest of these is love" (1 Cor. 13).

Where have you heard that before?

If you said "at a wedding" you are not alone. You've probably heard it at countless weddings, and maybe even your own. It's not bad advice. If you want a marriage to last you need to have patience, and kindness, and all the other things that 1 Corinthians 13 tells you about.

But there's a secret about that text. As much as we hear it at weddings, and as much as it gets engraved on everything from engagement rings to wedding invitations, it was not written about marriage. It wasn't even written about romantic love at all.

To understand, you have to go back to the source, and back to where this comes from, which is a letter sent by the Apostle Paul to the church in Corinth, a church he himself had founded and built up before moving on in his ministry. Paul is writing to them about a whole list of things that he thought they were doing wrong. In particular he's worried that they are fighting with each other and getting away from the things that he had taught them, especially teachings about God's love and about loving one another. That's the reason he writes them this letter that includes these famous words on what love is and what it is not.

When we read this today though, especially in English and without the rest of the letter or the context, it sounds like Paul is talking about romantic love or like it's the sort of thing you want to read at a wedding. But this text is about so much more than weddings; it's about being loved by God, and loving God.

Here's why I say that. In English, we really only have one word for "love." We love our spouses. We love our parents. We love our friends. We love our kids. We love God.

But in the language Paul was writing in, Greek, there's more than one word. There's *eros*, which is about romantic love. And there's *philos*, which is about brotherly love, like in the word "Philadelphia." And there's *storge*, which is about familial love.

But then there's this fourth word for love: *agape*. *Agape* is unlike any of the other kinds of love out there because *agape* is the kind of love that God has for us. Likewise, it is also the way that we in turn are called to love God.

When Paul wrote this letter it was *agape* that he was talking about, but *agape* gets a little lost in translation. *Agape* is not the kind of love you celebrate with red hearts on Valentine's Day. It's not even the kind you mean when you tell your family and friends you love them. It's a kind of love that is even more demanding, and more incredible, than that.

The first thing about *agape* love is that, like grace, it is not earned. God's *agape* love is for us, and it remains whether we love back or not. It's selfless. It's grace-filled. It's generous. And it's so hard to do well that probably the only one who has ever really done it consistently is God.

If you want to know more, just read the text again: "*Agape* is patient, *agape* is kind, *agape* bears all things, *agape* believes all things, *agape* hopes all things, *agape* endures all things . . . And now faith, hope, and *agape* abide, these three; and the greatest of these is *agape*."

In a real sense, this passage could be God's love letter to you. Paul is saying how much God loves you, and also how God loves you. God's love is *agape* love, and it doesn't get any better than that.

We began this book by asking about our purpose, and that's where we are finishing. When people ask me, "Why are we here?" or "What does it mean to be the church together?" the easiest answer I know is simply this: We are here to be loved by God, and we are here to love because of God. That's also discipleship and witnessing in a nutshell.

TIKKUN OLAM

It is my hope that everything we do as Christians is done because of *agape* love, both God's for us and ours for God. The first thing I think we are called to do as a church is to acknowledge that God loves us, and that God loves everyone. And in return, we are called to love God back with that same kind of fierce love.

The biggest part of the way we love God is by sharing God's love with others. The church does not exist for ourselves. We are here for all of God's creation. We are here for mission, and we are here to serve. We are here because the best way for us to love God is to love others.

To put it more succinctly, first we are loved, then we learn how to love, and then we love outside of ourselves.

When our *agape* love has no walls and when it has no boundaries, nothing is impossible with God. We can serve our hometowns, and we can serve our world. We can do big things and live in faith and not in fear. We can change lives, and we can do all of these things simply because God has loved us first.

This is what being a witness to the resurrection is all about. It's being a witness to the triumph of love over hatred, violence, and death. And it is how witnesses to the resurrection love God back: by loving the world boldly.

Our Jewish siblings have a phrase that I love to describe the work of actively loving all of creation: *tikkun olam*, which literally translates to "repair of the world." That resonates deeply with me. We live in a broken world, but it is still one we must love. The concept of *tikkun olam* teaches us that we can work with God to repair it. In a real way we are called to repair the world by loving it into wholeness.

While we who are Christians need to be careful not to appropriate an idea that is not our own, I believe that we can learn something from Jewish tradition here. The reality is that most faiths, in their truest form, teach something similar. That's why Muslims count the giving of *Zakat*, or the generous sharing of gifts with those in need, among the five pillars of the faith. And that's why *dana*, or generosity, is understood in Buddhist, Hindu, and Sikh traditions to be essential for the faithful.

In all of these traditions we are talking about more than charity, at least as we understand it in the modern sense. This isn't about throwing a couple of dollars into the donation buckets outside the mall at Christmas. Instead, this is active, continuing investment in a broken world. It is charity only in the sense of the original meaning of the word, the one that comes from *charis*, or grace. And for Christians it is the sharing of a grace that has been given generously to us.

Our work in the world, our grateful sharing of the grace we have received, is about loving a broken world enough to want to fix it. It's about continually trying, even though we know we never will quite succeed. Not entirely, anyway.

But because we are witnesses of the triumph of God's love over sure destruction, we know that our work in this life will never be entirely in vain. It can't be if we believe, in any way, that resurrection is true.

RELYING ON THE HOLY SPIRIT

You've already read about how some people call Christians "Easter peo-ple." We are; that's true. We live as people who know about the hope the Resurrection of Christ brings.

But what happens next? How do we live after the Resurrection?

The Book of Acts is like the biography of the early church. If you ever want to feel good about your all-too-human congregation, read the Book of Acts, and then read the letters sent by Paul and others to churches who just couldn't seem to get their stuff together. Church dys-function is a long tradition in Christianity.

One of the things I love most about Acts is how it starts: the disciples literally have their heads in the clouds. Acts tells us that Jesus was "lifted up" into the clouds. I'm not sure exactly what that looked like, but in the aftermath the disciples were left just standing around, looking up at the sky, and wondering what in the world just happened.

Scripture also tells us that while they were standing there two men in white approached and asked, essentially, "Why are you standing around with your heads in the clouds?"

The Book of Acts is about a group of people learning to get their heads out of the clouds and start being church together in new ways. They would have rather kept looking up and saying, "Now where did that guy with all the answers go?" But that's not what being a disciple is about. It's not about waiting for Jesus to descend from on high with all the answers. It's about getting to work.

That probably doesn't feel all that unfamiliar to those of us who are trying to be the church two thousand years later. Sometimes the church needs people like those two guys in white. We need them to call our at-tention back from gazing up at the clouds all the time and toward turning it to the world we are in now. We need them to remind us that we have a task here as disciples of Christ, because with the Ascension the baton has been passed; we are left as witnesses to Christ's life and work, and we are called to be the church.

And that's when Easter people have to become Pentecost people.

Pentecost Sunday is one of the hardest days of the church year to explain in a succinct way. That makes sense, because the Holy Spirit is the toughest aspect of the Trinity to understand. As much as humanly possible, we get God, the Father/Mother/Parent. And we get Jesus. But the Holy Spirit? Hard to define. Squishy. Amorphous.

And yet, the Holy Spirit is what made the first church get its act together. The Holy Spirit is also what the progressive church is going to need a little more of if we hope to do the work of repairing the world.

Picture this: It's ten days after Jesus' Ascension and the disciples are all together, trying to figure out what to do next now that Jesus is gone. All of a sudden a rushing wind, with tongues of fire, fell on them. And suddenly, the disciples, all of whom were Galileans who spoke the same language, were speaking languages that they had never known before. People from other places were nearby and they heard it and could understand what they were saying, and they asked "How come we are hearing this in our own language?"

Some didn't even believe it; they said that the disciples must be drunk. But Peter got up and said, "Look, it's only nine in the morning, . . . we're not drunk." Instead, something new had come, and everything has since changed.

In the church we call this the Pentecost, which is translated to mean "fifty days," as in fifty days after Easter. We call that mighty rush of wind that came down the coming of the Holy Spirit. Some even go so far as to call this the birthday of the church, saying this is the day when the gift of the Holy Spirit was given to the disciples, and the church was born.

I've always found that interesting. Because, intuitively, it might not make a lot of sense. Shouldn't Easter be the birthday of the church? After all, it's the day Jesus rose again and appeared to the disciples. Maybe you could even argue that Christmas, marking the birth of Christ, should be the day of celebration? Or maybe Maundy Thursday, when Jesus told the disciples how to love one another?

But most believe Pentecost is the church's birthday. I think it's because that was the day the disciples went from being this sort of loose band of followers of Jesus, standing around wondering "What now?" to being equipped by the Holy Spirit to serve not just themselves, but the whole world.

The Holy Spirit is what we in the church have to rely upon as we do the work of witnessing to God's love, and of engaging, and repairing, our world. We as Christians believe that God speaks to us and leads us through the Holy Spirit. It is our companion and guide through life. It is what gives us comfort when we need it and courage when we are done being comforted. Jesus even called the Holy Spirit "paraclete," which means "advocate" or "helper." And if ever the church, especially the progressive church, needed an advocate and guide in our work, it is now.

So if we are going to be Pentecost people in this broken world, if we are transformed disciples led by the Holy Spirit and witnessing to God's love and grace by transforming the world, how do we do it?

Here are the three thoughts on the "how" that I have for this point in our journey together: Be people of work, people of words, and people of joy.

GETTING OUR HEADS OUT OF THE CLOUDS

When the disciples got their heads out of the clouds, they got to work. That's good advice for progressive Christians because we spend a lot of our time navel gazing. We talk about church decline, and whether or not to sell our buildings, and what our new denominational structures will look like. We run to the next new church vitality prophet and listen for something that will "save" us. And then, when all of this fails to revive our churches, we do it again. It becomes an echo chamber, and we get so focused on ourselves that we get nothing done.

But when we are at our best, we become people of work.

The transformative work that the church is capable of doing, when we get our heads out of the clouds, is extraordinary. It's Karl Barth and Dietrich Bonhoeffer and the whole Confessing Church in Germany. It's the Dutch Reformed Church in South Africa writing the Belhar Confession, calling for the equality of all people, even while a system of apartheid still divided their country.

It's the work that's going on in your own churches too. Work like helping refugees to settle, advocating for better recovery treatment for people in the throes of addiction, feeding the hungry, fighting for a living wage, marching for peace, witnessing about gun violence, standing up to racism, or protecting the environment.

The progressive church has a special gift for confronting and dismantling structures of systemic sin. We are able to see the ways that society as a whole responds in sinful ways to the needs of our neighbors and all of creation. And, while we have to be careful not to lose sight of our own individual complicity in sin, it is the dismantling of these sinful structures that perhaps most benefits our world.

You may be saying at this point, "But we already do that. What's new here?"

My hope is that if you are already doing this work, you have already rooted it deeply in the love of God. I hope you do the work of transforming the world because you know that you yourself have been transformed by the grace of God, and you want to witness to God's love. I hope these things, because I know that this is hard work, and I know that without a solid foundation in which this work is planted, it is all too easy to burn out. The world needs us too much for us to burn out.

H. Richard Niebuhr wrote that, contrary to most Christians' views, Christ had the power to do more than just be against culture, of culture, above culture, or held in paradox to culture. Instead, Christ transforms culture. That is, Christ is still actively involved in the work of the world, and is actively transforming it.

We know that's true because Christ actively transformed, and still transforms, us. And if that's true, it means our work is rooted in a power far greater than ourselves, one that will sustain us in our greatest challenges. Our work is to engage the world with the same kind of transformative love with which Christ engaged us, and to follow Christ boldly into a world in which he is already at work.

IF NECESSARY, USE WORDS

St. Francis has been credited with a quote that has gained popularity with progressive Christians: "Preach the gospel at all times, and, if necessary, use words." While that quote may certainly be true to the Franciscan spirit, it probably wasn't said by Francis himself. In fact, St. Francis was known for being quite an effective preacher (the kind who uses words).

There's something about that quote that we progressive Christians seem to love, though, myself included. I think part of it is that it lets us off the hook. If we can preach our faith only by our deeds, then we don't have to do the hard work of talking about it. Let's admit it; none of us wants to sound like a religious fanatic, and that's exactly what we are afraid will happen if we start talking about God and Jesus all the time.

But as much as words scare us, the faith still demands them, especially of Pentecost people. I think it says a lot that on that day when the Holy Spirit came down, the first gift that the disciples realize they have is the gift of being able to speak in new languages, and to translate the message to others.

There's something particular about that, though. Do you notice something about the Pentecost story? When the Holy Spirit comes, it's the disciples who learn the new language. All the other people there don't suddenly speak the disciples' language; instead the disciples have to learn to speak theirs.

I think maybe the Holy Spirit is trying to tell us something. We can't wait for others to talk the way we talk. Instead, we have to learn their language. We have to learn what is important to them. We have to be able to communicate in the ways that matter to them. We have to be willing to make the connections. It's what the church has been doing since its first days, and it's what we are still called to do today.

And, more importantly, we have to have something to say.

As I said at the beginning of this book, one of my greatest fears about us as progressive Christians is that we are more apt to proclaim the Gospel of Why We Are Different from Other Christians than the Gospel of Jesus Christ. We define ourselves by the negative, and are so quick to say we're "not all like that." And, sure, it's a good thing that people know not all Christians believe the same thing. But saying "not all Christians" is not the same as proclaiming the gospel (which is a calling of every Christian, lay or ordained).

Even if that favorite quote is to be believed, it still says "if necessary, use words." I would submit that at this point in the progressive church's life, words are necessary. We can no longer allow only others to speak on behalf of the name Christian. Instead, we must reclaim our public witness in new and creative ways. We need progressive Christians who write, speak, sing, play, and paint their faith. We need Christian leaders who can speak effectively about who Jesus is to them as they take prophetic public stands. We need to be able to glorify God with all of us, including our words.

Jesus once asked Peter, "Who do you say that I am?" Peter first responded by giving Jesus the answer he had heard from everyone else: "Some say this, Jesus, . . . others say that." Jesus asked again, "But who do *you* say that I am?"

"You are the Messiah," said Peter. "The Lord."

Every person who would follow Christ should be prepared to answer that question in their own way. Each of our answers will be a little different, but if they come from our faith, they will be enough. And when the people in our lives ask us "why" we follow this Jesus guy, and why we live our lives the way we do, our answers can do more than just describe Christians in a different way. Our words can describe God's love in ways that are so extraordinary, even in their simplicity, that we just might find that our friends and neighbors have been waiting their whole lives to hear them.

ENJOY GOD FOREVER

Karl Barth once wrote that "joy is the simplest form of gratitude."[13] He also wrote that "laughter is the closest thing to the grace of God."[14]

If that's true, then why are Christians generally regarded as such a dour bunch?

I'll confess that even I have thought of Christians that way. And when I'm visiting a church and walk in on Sunday morning, if I can't sense any kind of palpable joy it's hard for me to even sit there for the service. Why? Because if I can't sense any joy in a congregation, I wonder whether the gospel is being preached there at all.

Let me be clear again, as I was in an earlier chapter, that joy is different from just being happy. I have been at devastatingly tragic funerals where joy was nonetheless at least still present at moments. And I've known joy even in the midst of times of deep sorrow. Joy is not about everything being okay. Joy, at a basic level, is about the hope that God's love is capable of transforming everything, even us.

God's glory and our joy cannot be separated from one another. Because God is worthy of being glorified, we who are God's creation can find joy. And, conversely, because we can find joy, we know that God is worthy of glory.

And so, in a real way, I hope that you are about to either begin, or continue on, a journey of joy, and I pray that as you seek to glorify God, you will enjoy life in a new and deeper way. And because of this, I hope that you will further glorify God by living your life in a way that it may bring joy, real joy, to others.

This is a journey that never ends. It's a sort of praxis where we will continually deepen our discipleship, and then deepen our witness in the world. The two will inform and feed one another, and together they will push us onward.

We are people of purpose. We are people of transformation. And we are people who are called to be transformative. But most of all, we are people who have received truly amazing grace, and people who cannot help but to now live and act with grateful hearts in every part of our lives.

To God be the glory, and to all of us be the joy.

Epilogue: Let it Shine

INITIATORS

The best story I know about hope and fear comes from the book of Exodus, and especially the story of the crossing of the Red Sea. I'm not talking about the Charlton Heston-as-Moses version here, where there are these really bad 1950s special effects and the waters peel back and Moses and the people can see clear across to the other shore. In the movie they all look amazed and start shouting, "It's a miracle." They run through before the waters close back up again and they are then saved from Pharaoh's army.

That's the way it happens in the movie. But I've always believed that the book is better than the movie, and the Bible is no exception.

Exodus tells us about a people who are hopeful enough to start out on a journey but realistic enough to be scared. They have left behind all they knew, which wasn't good, but which now seems a whole lot better than this new reality where they are stuck in the wilderness and facing what seems like certain death. So it's understandable that they start to wonder why they ever followed this Moses guy anyway.

I'm sure that if I had been there, I'd be doubting all of this too. I'd be wondering whether it might be better to give up hope and to just go back to what I'd always known. That's because hope can be dangerous sometimes. It can put us in situations we never dreamed of, and it can make us wonder why we ever dared to think we could do something new.

That's what was happening that day as they stood on the banks of the water. The loss of hope, the triumph of doubt, the fear. They were all there.

In the movie version, that all only lasts a few seconds. Moses turns around and parts the waters and it is so breathtakingly awesome that doubt vanishes just like that. The people cross over and they know, for at least a little while anyway, that God is with them. How could they doubt after seeing something like that?

But have you ever wondered whether that was how it really happened?

Rabbis have a tradition of Scripture study called Midrash. It's a way of taking a particular story from the biblical text and thinking over and wondering about the meaning, including those things that are left unspoken. There's one particular interpretation in this wonderful Midrashic tradition about this text, which, in my mind at least, is ten times better than the movie.

In this interpretation, there is a man who is mentioned in the Book of Exodus who is named "Nahshon." And when Moses calls on God to part the Red Sea, as this version of the story goes, it doesn't automatically part. Instead, everyone stands there wondering why nothing is happening. But then Nahshon steps out into the water. First one step. Then another. The water gets up to his ankles, up to his knees, up to his hips and shoulders. And finally, when it is up to his nose, the water finally parts.

I like that telling of the story because I believe that God could have parted those waters in one fell swoop. I believe that the Israelites could have seen the shore and known that they were going to be safe from the get-go. But I believe that sometimes God asks us to show a little bit of faith, and a little bit of commitment.

Sometimes God wants us to be a Nahshon, and so God lets us get nose-deep in the waters. That's not because God is toying with us, or being sadistic. Instead, that's because God is preparing us for something better. God is using our faith and our hope to shape us and to teach us that our actions, our responses, matter too.

The name "Nahshon" is sometimes used to mean "an initiator." That's what he did that day. He took the initiative and started the crossing. And there are some who push this text even further and say that even after he got nose deep, and even after the sea started to part, it was a gradual process. The people took one step, and a little more of the sea parted. And then another, and it parted more. And another, and another, trusting that if they just took the next right step, God would show them the next place after that. And eventually, God would lead them to dry ground.

When you think about it, that's what the journey of faith is like. We don't get to see the end. We don't get to see dry land on our first step. But sometimes we get to see just enough to know where to take the next right step. And then we step out in faith believing that God won't leave us stranded, and that the waters will not overpower us. We step out believing that God will make a way.

AN OPEN DOOR

Carved in stone on the front of Old South Church in Boston is this inscription from the book of Revelation: "Behold, I Set Before Thee an Open Door."

I walked through the doors under those words many times, but I never noticed them until the night I proposed to my now wife. It was not long after I had gotten down on one knee and she had said "yes" that we were standing in front of the church, a few days before Christmas with the streets of Boston filled with light.

I had been scared to death to propose. Not because I thought Heidi would say "no," but because I knew everything was about to change.

And as wonderful as I knew that was going to be, it was also terrifying . . . because change is always terrifying.

That's when I looked up, and read those words, and I knew that a whole new, wonderful chapter of life was beginning. The door was being held open, and though I didn't know exactly what was on the other side, I knew it was time to take that first step through. It was time to take put a foot in the water and to wait for God to show me the next right step.

I think we all have times in our life where we have to decide to take the first step. We have moments when we are asked to initiate something new. If we are being honest with ourselves, those moments can fill us with fear. But at the same time, they can be the start of something wonderful.

God is constantly at work in the church, just as God is constantly at work in the world. We who are the church have a choice; we can join in the unending work of reformation, or we can stay on the shore of fear and caution, never daring to put our feet in the water.

The paradox is that when we become unwilling to be moved and transformed, we are not saving ourselves. Quite to the contrary, we are giving up. But the good news is that God has set an open door before us. It's waiting, and whatever is behind the door is good. We know that because, whatever it is, God is there.

I don't know what the progressive church will look like in ten years, or twenty, or a century. But I do know that, whatever it is, Christ will be at the heart of it, and God's love and grace will define it. And I know that where God is glorified, and where God's people live in joy, that is where the church will thrive.

Now is the time, progressive Christians. The light of Christ can burn brightly in all of us. And we can let it shine.

Notes

1. Statistics in this section are from Michael Lipka, "Mainline Protestants make up shrinking number of U.S. adults," Pew Research Center FactTank, May 18, 2015, http://www.pewresearch.org/fact-tank/2015/05/18/mainline-protestants-make-up-shrinking-number-of-u-s-adults/.

2. Tracy Chapman, "Change," *Where You Live* 2005 © Elektra Records.

3. J. K. Rowling, *Very Good Lives: The Fringe Benefits of Failure and the Importance of Imagination*, (New York: Little, Brown, 2015), 33.

4. Robert D. Putnam, *Bowling Alone* (New York: Simon & Schuster, 2000), 112.

5. Ibid., 438–44.

6. Robert Putnam and Thomas Sanders, "Still Bowling Alone? The Post-9/11 Split" *Journal of Democracy* vol. 21:1 (January 2010): 11.

7. Ibid., 9–10.

8. David Briggs, "Parents are top influence in teens remaining active in religion as young adults," *Christian Century* (Nov. 5, 2014), 17–18.

9. Bob Dylan, "Gotta Serve Somebody," *Slow Train Coming*, © 1979 Special Rider Music.

10. *Calvin: Institutes of Christian Religion: Volume I,* ed. John T. McNeill (Philadelphia: Westminster, 1960), 35.

11. C. S. Lewis, *Mere Christianity* (New York: Harper Collins, 1952, 1980), 175.

12. "Barmen Declaration," *Book of Confessions*, study edition (Louisville: Geneva Press, 1996), 311.

13. As quoted in Bob Stromberg, *Finding the Magnificent in Lower Mundane* (Grand Rapids, MI: Zondervan, 1994), 69.

14. As quoted in Robert I. Fitzhenry, ed., *The Harper Book of Quotations* (New York: HarperPerennial, 1993), 223.